MODELLING RAILWAY SCENERY

MODELLING RAILWAY SCENERY

VOLUME I
CUTTINGS, HILLS, MOUNTAINS, STREAMS AND LAKES

ANTHONY REEVES

THE CROWOOD PRESS

First published in 2013 by
The Crowood Press Ltd
Ramsbury, Marlborough
Wiltshire SN8 2HR

www.crowood.com

British Library Cataloguing-in-Publication Data
A catalogue record for this book is available from the British Library.

ISBN 978 1 84797 619 2

Dedication
For Nic, Luke, Libby and Benson
and my family, past, present and future.
'Take a look around and enjoy every day.'

Acknowledgements
The author and publisher would like to thank the following companies for their generous support in the making of this book: A K Interactive, Deluxe materials, Javis Manufacturing Ltd, Noch, P&D Marsh Model Railways, Treemendus.

Disclaimer
The author and the publisher do not accept any responsibility in any manner whatsoever for any error or omission, or any loss, damage, injury, adverse outcome, or liability of any kind incurred as a result of the use of any of the information contained in this book, or reliance upon it. If in doubt about any aspect of scenic modelling, readers are advised to seek professional advice.

Typeset in Gill Sans by Bookcraft Ltd, Stroud, Gloucestershire
Printed and bound in India by Gopsons Papers Ltd

CONTENTS

SCENERY n.

1. the general appearance of the natural … features of a landscape, esp. when picturesque.

2. (Theatre) the painted representations of landscape, rooms, etc., used as the background … in a play etc.

INTRODUCTION – SETTING THE SCENE

STARTING OUT

Being born in 1967, I missed out on the steam era of British railways, growing up in a time of diesel and electric locomotives. In recent years, a number of the classes from my era have also been consigned to the history books. One element of rail travel that does stay more constant, however, is the countryside through which the trains pass. I have always had a fascination with all elements of railway scenery, both in the real world and in the scale-model world. It is fascinating how the landscape, structures and railways have a profound effect on each other.

I was given my first 'train set' as a gift in 1977, the year of the Queen's Silver Jubilee and a great year for music too. It was the Hornby InterCity 125 (HST) set, which, if I remember rightly, consisted of two power cars, one for each end of the train, with a single carriage plonked in between them. The set also contained an oval of track, battery power module, power clip, uncoupling ramp and a cardboard tunnel. It was the tunnel that, even at the age of ten, I found to be the least acceptable item – a foot-long arch of cardboard that served no purpose at all. I doubt if mine ever graced the oval of track more than once.

On reflection, it was actually that cardboard tunnel that was the biggest inspiration of the whole train set, as it led me to make my own tunnels on a scenic baseboard for my new train to chase its tail around. Over time, more track was added, to create a double track oval with a couple of points for the train to switch tracks. A few sidings were added towards the front. This was pinned to an

Fig. 1. Railways run through diverse surroundings, from stunningly beautiful scenery to the most built-up industrial areas of Britain.

Fig. 2. Two power cars are all that remain from that original HST set.

8 x 4ft chipboard base. The base was split down its centre lengthways with an imaginary line, and two plastic moulded tunnel mouths were added, one at each end of the oval.

From that point I was free to create my first scenic baseboard. I used chicken wire to make a hillside that joined the two tunnel mouths together. This hillside is what separated the front 'scenic side' of the layout from the 'fiddle yard' at the rear of the layout. Looking back, it may have been a waste of space to have included a fiddle yard on the layout as no one but me and a few family and friends would ever see it. However, I wanted to give the impression that the trains were actually going somewhere when they entered the tunnels and returning from some far-flung part of the country when they reappeared, not just going round and round the same track.

This all happened thirty-five years ago. These days, of course, there is a far wider choice of scenic modelling materials available. Nonetheless, some of the basic building materials and principles I used then are still in use today.

Concentrating on the scenery of what became much more than a 'train set' – once I had given it my attention, it had become a 'model railway' – completely took over from running the trains. I enjoyed and learnt so much from my early experiences that, when the layout was 'finished', I took it up and reworked the whole setting. My passion for the scenic elements of railway modelling eventually led me to develop the Treemendus range of scenic modelling materials, which are used today by modellers worldwide.

EARLY INSPIRATION

Most of my childhood weekends and school holidays were spent in our local woods and surrounding areas, climbing trees, bird watching and taking in the sights and smells of natural open places. I have always had a fascination with the way trees and plants grow, the way they interact with each other and their ever-changing forms and colours. As I walk our dog Benson every day, usually down the same lane towards the river Mersey, the shape, colour and quantity of the plants around us seem to change almost on a daily basis. As old plants die back, new ones spurt into growth to replace them. Depending on the atmospheric conditions, colours change, seemingly before our very eyes. Streams and rivers always seem to find the most convenient route and are very much affected by what lies under the ground as, over time, they cut their way through the landscape. Altitude and the harsh elements in mountainous areas have a

Fig. 3. Traditional British countryside, showing the incredible variety of colours and textures.

huge effect on the appearance and characteristics of the way things grow and die.

It is important to remember that much of the scenery you will be creating for your model railway is quite literally as old as the hills. It was there long before the railways. Railways were built over streams, under hills, around lakes and through mountains because they had to be. If you can replicate this in any way in your models, it will give a better impression of the prototype. It can also be used to your advantage. Remember the cardboard tunnel? It served no real purpose, but if you put a tunnel mouth at the point just before the spur enters the fiddle yard, it can deceive the eye and therefore the brain into thinking that the train has entered a tunnel that *had* to be put there so that the train could continue on its journey.

Cuttings, trees and of course buildings can be used in much the same way – to hide the exit point of a train from the scenic layout. The eye may also be deceived by subtle colour changes within a layout. Colour fades with distance, so if, as in nature, the 'near' views are made a touch brighter and more colourful than the 'distant' views, the mind can be tricked into believing there is more space in the field of view than there actually is. Importantly, as the colour fades with distance so does the apparent size of features in the landscape. Trees and other

features which are to be placed towards the rear of the layout should be made slightly smaller than the same features at the foreground of the scene. This is where artistic licence comes into play. You may want to model a huge tree in the distance but only require small trees at the front, so naturally the distant tree could appear larger than the foreground trees. There will be occasions when you see features just asking to be modelled.

Fig. 4. Features such as this will add character to your layouts and are easy to build from scratch.

RESEARCH YOUR LOCATION

FIELD TRIPS

A field trip to the location you intend to model is recommended in order to gain a feel for the area in question. If possible, more than one field trip is even better. If you are working on a layout where the prototype still exists, a train journey through your chosen area will help enormously. If you go during the time of year on which your layout will be based, you can see for yourself exactly how the surrounding hills, mountains, streams, lakes all interact to create the unique scenery that makes up your chosen area. This is assuming you are modelling a location with a picturesque rural setting but the same applies for layouts based on an industrial location. There is no substitute for actually seeing the area you are modelling 'in the flesh'.

The reasoning behind this is that the geology of countryside changes dramatically from one part of the country to another and this affects the appearance of what is seen above the ground. The Cornish Riviera is very different in appearance from the North Yorkshire Moors, neither of them look like the Scottish Highlands. If you can capture some of the attributes that go into making each of these areas what they are, you can present a convincing scale model which oozes all the character of the area being modelled.

Fig. 5. Take care when on field trips and take your litter home with you.

> ### Beware of trains!
>
> Always remember that railways can be dangerous places so take care when doing your research and always ask permission from the landowner where necessary.

PHOTOGRAPHIC REFERENCES

When on location take as many colour photographs as you possibly can. In these days of digital cameras you can get literally hundreds at a time and these will be the references from which you work for a long time to come. Try to take some photographs of the area from a fair distance too, as this will give you a good indication of what the surroundings may look like scaled down in model form.

It is also very important to remember that people see and react to colour in different ways. I tend to tone my colours down a little so they do not appear too gaudy but in reality some grasses for instance can be of the brightest green. Remember also that you are creating a 'work of art'. That is not to say that you expect it to be put on public display, but it will nonetheless be a piece of work that involves artistry. For this reason, you should aim to add your own interpretation, in order to create unique scenic models for your railways to run through.

Detailed research can really help in creating an authentic model of a particular location or general area. If, for whatever reason, you cannot get to your chosen area, do not be too disheartened. Although it is best to see the real thing, a search online should show you what you need to see. Similarly, if you are modelling a specific rural station, which may no longer exist, you may need to use the internet in order to find out what buildings were adjacent to it, what animals were kept in the surrounding fields, or what the row of trees looked like standing behind the platform. You should be able to find all sorts of information online, often with photographic evidence to help you.

While research is important, you should also be prepared to use a bit of artistic licence. If something looks right and sits right within the landscape I am creating I am usually happy to let it go. Above all, creating model railway scenery should be fun and bring you enjoyment.

USING THIS BOOK

The chapters of this book cover a series of easy-to-follow step-by-step scenic diorama builds, each concentrating on a particular aspect of railway scenery – cuttings, hills, mountains, streams and lakes. Others are included that do not necessarily relate to railways. It is important to imagine the different elements as being part of the same landscape. For example, a stream makes its way from the rocky mountain top to form a small waterfall, which then meanders down a gentle hillside and ultimately ends up joining a lake. Each chapter contains informative text and a series of photographs that highlight the techniques of each stage. The step-by-step instructions and photographs will assist you in tackling some of the problems modellers encounter and help to answer many of the questions that I am asked at trade shows.

This book is aimed at modellers who have some experience of railway modelling and, although it does not exclude newcomers to the hobby, it does not cover baseboard construction, track laying or electrics. Its emphasis is on creating beautifully realistic, convincing scale-model scenery. The dioramas are built to 1:76 (4mm to the foot) or 00-gauge, which is the most popular scale in the UK for railway modelling. The same techniques and materials used in creating 00-gauge model railways are suitable for whichever scale you choose to work in; they simply need to be scaled up or down appropriately.

It is also fair to say that, for all but the very fortunate, space will be a major consideration when embarking on a model railway project. This can have a bearing on the scale that you choose. If you envisage your layout as having huge hillsides or mountains and valleys with sweeping curves of track, then one of the smaller gauges will be an obvious choice.

MATERIALS AND TOOLS

Each chapter starts with a basic materials and tools list. These lists are not exhaustive and other materials will be used during the building process. Not all the detailing materials are included but they are covered in the text.

Fig. 6. A small sample of construction materials.

Fig. 7. Good-quality groundwork materials are essential in the creation of convincing scale-model scenery.

CONSTRUCTION MATERIALS

The 'construction' materials used to make the dioramas include polystyrene, chicken wire, cardboard, wood, cement, PVA glue, cork sheet and ceiling tiles. Some of these can be substituted by other materials and recommendations are given where possible.

GROUNDWORK MATERIALS

The 'groundwork' materials – for hedges, trees, earth, grass and foliage – including scatters, earth powders, grass fabric and other materials, come from the Treemendus Scenic Modelling Materials range. There are a vast range of scenic modelling materials from different manufacturers on the market and some of these will be introduced into the dioramas as they progress.

TOOLS

A basic tool kit will comprise a sharp scalpel or craft knife, steel rule, sharp scissors, wire cutters, assorted paintbrushes and paints, and hairspray. Reference is given in each chapter to the specific tools needed to complete each stage of the build.

METHODS USED

The techniques involved vary from build to build but there is also some repetition from chapter to chapter. Reference is made if the same technique is used elsewhere in the book, with the aim of inspiring consistency in your scenic modelling.

Although the models featured in this book are small dioramas, the methods used will relate directly to larger-sized model railway layouts. The text assumes that bare baseboards with track laid are in place.

CHECKLIST

The railways were built through an existing landscape and it is very important to bear this in mind when creating your model railway. With careful planning, this fact can be effectively replicated. Some of the

Fig. 8. A selection of the tools you will need.

features of the landscaping process may also be used to your advantage, for example, when it comes to disguising exit points on your models.

Going on field trips and taking lots of reference photographs is a very important part of the planning process if you want to create a faithful representation of an actual location. It is less important if you are building a general scenic layout, but it is still well worth looking at some actual railway lines and their surrounding area. This will give you a feel for the colours and the way the features of the railway interact with each other and the landscape.

Landscapes change all the time and are significantly affected by the seasons and the weather. The way you use colour will make your models original and unique and the colour values you choose will tell the viewer about the time of year being portrayed in a particular scene.

Use the vast amounts of information available on the internet where necessary. During the course of building your model there will be many times when you need more references, so make sure you use this valuable tool.

With the necessary construction materials, a supply of quality groundwork materials and a sensible collection of tools, you are ready to embark on your journey.

CHAPTER ONE

STONE-LINED CUTTINGS

Fig. 9. Weathered stone blocks photographed in Cheshire.

Materials

- Strawboard (3mm thick) or ply board
- Pine strip wood
- Plastic (or paper) brick/stone effect sheets
- PVA glue
- Newspaper or chicken wire
- Cement or plaster
- Hairspray
- Scenic modelling materials (from Treemendus; see text)
- Emulsion paints
- Paints/weathering powders (from AK Interactive)

Tools

- Steel rule
- Pen/pencil
- Scalpel/Stanley knife
- Cutting board
- Assorted paintbrushes

Most railway journeys will at some stage involve travelling through a man-made trough or 'cutting'. Cuttings are a vital part of the railway infrastructure – following the most direct route from station to station often results in the need to take the line straight through a solid hillside, using cuttings and tunnels. Branch lines, which go from a main railway station to a countryside area or small town, will almost invariably pass through at least one cutting, large or small.

There are many cuttings in the UK and overseas that are blasted and carved out of solid rock. Once the loose rocks and debris have been removed, the walls of some of these cuttings are still strong enough to hold themselves up. Cuttings made through less stable ground are excavated in the same way, but they need to be lined with stone or brick walls. This enables all the loose earth to be held back, much like any retaining wall but generally on a much larger scale. There is much that could be written about large gravity-retaining walls and how they are built and work, but here the concern is only to make a realistic scale model.

CREATING CUTTING WALLS

PLANNING AND PREPARATION

With a bit of planning, it can be quite simple to create realistic-looking cutting walls.

Cuttings vary in height enormously – some are very shallow while others are very deep and dwarf the trains that run through them. The first step of planning is to decide how tall your walls are to be. Remember that a cutting can start out relatively shallow and gain in depth as the hill through which it has been built gets steeper, and the walls should reflect this. A cutting like this often leads to a tunnel mouth.

This project uses 3mm thick strawboard for the wall, but corrugated cardboard is good too, being very lightweight and easy to trim and bend. Ply board is another useful option and has the benefit of being strong yet fairly flexible. This is particularly useful where retaining walls are to be built on curves. When building walls on curves using thick card, it is recommended to score the front or rear side of the card with vertical scores to allow it to bend more easily. Score the front of the card for walls on the inside of a bend and score the rear side of the card for walls to the outside of the bend. Scoring also helps the walls stay in position while the glue that holds it in place dries. It also helps to curb the natural tendency of the card to spring back to its original flat form.

It is worthwhile measuring and cutting the whole length of wall needed for the project at this stage, so that all the lengths can, if necessary, be trimmed to exactly the same height. This makes for a neater-looking wall once the coping stones are attached. It is also a good time to mark and cut the pillars that can be seen on the prototype wall. These pillars strengthen the wall.

MEASURING AND CUTTING

Use a steel rule to carefully measure and mark on the card or ply board all the components of the wall (Fig. 10). If for any reason the height of your retaining wall is critical, it is worth bearing in mind that coping stones will be added to the top of the wall during its

Fig. 10. Take time to get your measurements as accurate as possible.

construction, although for 1:76 scale these will only be 2–3mm in thickness so will not really affect the overall height.

The height of this wall is 101mm. It consists of a lower section of wall measuring 80mm in height, a 3mm thick card plinth, a 15mm high upper wall section and, to top it off, coping stones made using 3mm thick strawboard. The pillars measure 110mm in height. The pillars are cut from 12 x 15mm pine strip wood, with the 15mm face towards the front. The distance between each pillar is 250mm. These measurements are by no means an industry standard;

Fig. 11. Carefully trim out all the components.

> **Tip**
>
> Always take great care when using sharp blades for cutting out components. It is better to take your time and do more shallow cuts rather than trying to cut through it in one. Keep the blade as vertical as possible to give nice square edges.

> **Tip**
>
> It is very important to lay the plastic sheet face down and have the rear side of the wall sections face up as you trim. This ensures that the correct face of the stone sheet will be facing outwards after trimming (another good reason to mark the card front and back.

dimensions undoubtedly change to fit each individual cutting in the real world.

Having carefully marked all the components for the wall on the card, the next stage is to cut them out using a scalpel or Stanley knife (Fig. 11).

Measure, mark and cut the pillars to length, keeping the blade nice and square. The timber used for the pillars is 15 x 12mm pine strip wood available from any DIY superstore. You might find it useful to mark the card so that you can tell at a glance which is the front and back. This is particularly useful if you are making a long length of retaining wall, as the pieces can soon add up.

The next step is to trim the embossed stone sheets to size (Fig. 12). This sheet is actually a 1:43 scale sheet but works perfectly well for this sort of application in 1:76 scale modelling. The best way to do this is to place the trimmed cardboard pieces (cut out in the previous step) over the plastic sheet.

Fig. 12. Trimming the embossed sheet.

Although it may not be apparent at this stage, it is a good idea to trim some strips of card to act as spacers at the bottom of the wall. These can be used to cause the wall to lean back as it rises away from ground level, creating a realistic angle to it. For this reason, when trimming the plastic sheet for the lower wall section, allow 2mm overhang from one of the long edges of the card. This will cut down on the gap between the bottom of the wall and the baseboard. In this wall the lower section of wall is 80mm, so the plastic sheet is cut at 82mm.

Trim around the wooden pillars by placing the wood on the plastic sheet and cutting around it with a sharp blade. Alternatively, take the measurements of the wood and mark them on the plastic sheet and then trim the pieces out. It is advisable to trim the stone sheet for the front of the pillars fractionally wider than the wood itself, as this will help hide any gaps at the corners of the pillars.

Printed paper sheets can be an effective way of representing walls and there is a huge choice of brick styles available. If you decide to use printed paper sheets for your wall, cut the paper 20mm or so larger than the section of wall you are covering. Apply glue to the front, edges and around the edges on the back of the card. Lay the printed sheet face down on a hard flat surface and carefully put the pre-glued section of card in the centre of it, with the front of the wall facing down. This will leave an overhang of paper all the way around the card. Cut a wedge shape out from the corners to create flaps, then pull and fold the flaps around the edges of the card and flatten them onto the glue. Any bubbles on the front of the wall can be removed by pricking the

Fig. 13. Even short lengths of wall can use a lot of individual pieces.

paper with a pin and smoothing over with a finger to force out the air. Once the components have been created, the wall can be constructed following the steps below, but without the need to use plastic embossed sheets. There are many components that can go into building even a short length of simple retaining wall (Fig. 13). Set these pieces to one side whilst the baseboard is prepared for them.

POSITIONING AND CONSTRUCTION

Assuming you already have your track work in place, it is important before positioning anything else on the boards that the correct clearance is left for all current stock, as well as any you may run in the future (Fig. 14). One way of doing this is to hold a pencil or marker pen to the side of a long-wheel-based carriage and run this around the track. This way you will know that anything built outside the line is not going to interfere with the running of any stock. As this diorama is only a short length of straight track, a wagon was used.

The red crayon line drawn above the track indicates the closest point to the track where anything can be safely positioned without obstructing the running of stock (Fig. 15). The red line therefore indicates the position of the front of the wall's pillars. Behind the pillar will be a length of 3mm strawboard (ply board could be used here instead). This length

Fig. 14. It is important to make sure the cutting wall will not obstruct any stock you are planning to run.

of card will be a little lower than the final height of the wall; all the components prepared earlier will be attached to it. Marked at the back is the gluing position for the wooden blocks that will hold the wall upright and in place. (There are simpler ways of measuring the position of these wooden blocks, but this image aims to show the logic behind it.) (See line drawing on page 18.)

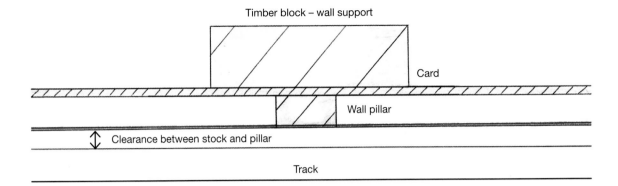

Timber block – wall support

Card

Wall pillar

Clearance between stock and pillar

Track

Fig. 15. Make sure everything has been taken into account before gluing anything down.

Fig. 16. Wooden blocks help support the wall.

Fig. 17. Creating an orderly way of working really does help.

Fig. 18. Construction of the wall can now begin.

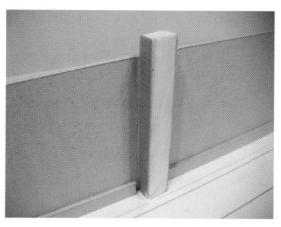

Fig. 19. With the pillars in place the stonework can be added.

Another red line drawn along the length of track shows where all the wall supports should be placed (Fig. 16). Small timber blocks have been glued along its length using PVA adhesive. When the blocks are set a supporting wall is glued in place on to the front of them. This 'wall' should be about 10mm lower than the height of the finished wall. A bead of PVA is run along the red line at the base of the blocks, to ensure maximum adhesion and support.

It is a good idea to lay out all the components in their correct position before starting any final gluing (Fig. 17). This orderly way of working allows you to clarify which pieces go where, and also helps to avoid that blind panic moment when nothing seems to fit together and everything ends up covered in glue.

Once the supporting wall has thoroughly dried, the time has come to build the wall for real (Fig. 18). Using PVA, glue in position one of the pillars and then measure and mark the distance to the next pillar. It can be useful to use the pre-cut section of lower wall as a measuring guide as opposed to a ruler. Continue this step until all the pillars are glued in place. Note that thin strips of card have been glued to the wall between the pillars at ground level. This is what will create a batter to the wall.

When the pillars have set in place, the embossed sheet can be added (Fig. 19). By gluing the sides of the pillar on first and the front on last, it is easier to

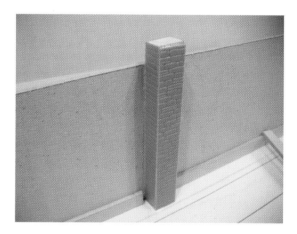

Fig. 20. Line up the courses of stone – this adds to the realism of the wall.

hide any gaps that may appear. Remember too that the front pieces of the plastic sheet have been cut slightly wider than the width of the wood. PVA may be used to hold the plastic sheet in place but you could use superglue or a grab adhesive.

The next step involves adding the embossed plastic sheet to the front of the pillar (Fig. 20). It is important to get the courses of the stonework to line up horizontally as this will add to the realism of the courses of stone in the wall. Any small gaps can

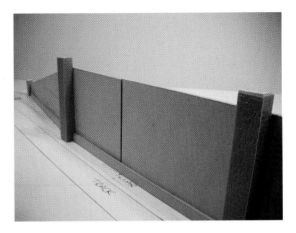

Fig. 21. All the pillars are dressed.

be filled in with filler, although the painting process that comes at the end can be used to cover small imperfections.

Add stonework to all the pillars and to the lower sections of walling (Figs 21 and 22). Note how the pillars do not come beyond the red line drawn at the beginning of the planning stage. Remember to leave a 2mm overhang on the long edge that meets the baseboard. Quick-drying Speed Bond from Deluxe Materials is used to fix the wall sections to each other, but superglue or grab adhesive can also be used for this stage of the construction.

With the pillars and lower sections of walling in place, it is apparent how effective a simple card spacer is at giving the wall a convincing angle as it rises (Fig. 23). Note too there is no gap between the bottom of the wall and the baseboard – this is down to the slight overhang of the plastic sheet. If there is a slight gap, it will easily be hidden at the groundwork stages of the scenic work, which will be carried out later.

A card plinth (something for the pigeons to sit on) can be added between the lower and upper wall sections, using plastic or balsa wood (Fig. 24). Although this is not critical, it is the sort of little detail that will add to the overall appearance of the finished wall.

The next step is to glue the upper section of wall into position (Fig. 25). Note how this section is vertical as no spacer has been glued to the supporting wall. Work along the length of wall until all the sections are in place. Once all the sections of stonework walling are present and in place (Fig. 26), it becomes clear how careful cutting at the beginning of the project can keep gaps to a minimum. Even if there are any imperfections at this stage, the painting process that comes later should hide them all.

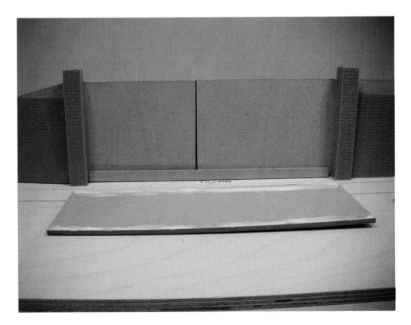

Fig. 22. The lower wall sections are added.

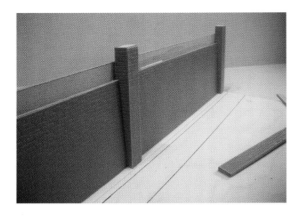

Fig. 23. Note the batter of the wall due to the card spacer glued to the bottom of the supporting wall.

Fig. 24. A little detail being added to the wall.

Fig. 25. The upper sections of wall are glued vertically.

Fig. 26. Almost finished.

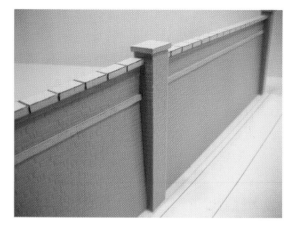

Fig. 27. The pillars are topped off with capping stones.

Final touches are added to the wall in the form of coping stones (Fig. 27), made from card (as here), or plastic or balsa. The individual stones are roughly marked using a biro, which will be almost lost under a coat of paint and some weathering at a later stage.

Once all the wall sections are in place they should be allowed to dry. This method of building retaining walls results in a very strong structure and the same principles can be used in the construction of tunnel mouths and, indeed, buildings for the layout.

LANDSCAPING

Looking at the rear of the retaining wall (Fig. 28), it is clear how the supporting wall is glued to the wooden blocks and is lower than the coping stones. Work has also started on the construction of the hill through which the cutting has been built. Again, 3mm strawboard has been used for this diorama but ply board could also be used on a layout. Wedge-shaped pieces of card have been cut to hold the back of the hill in place. However, wooden blocks could be used instead, as they were for the retaining wall. PVA was used to hold all this in place.

The back of this particular hill could very well meet the back scene of a layout and the cutting itself could lead to a tunnel, which is a scenic break between the layout and a fiddle yard.

To create support for the hard surface of the land, screwed-up newspaper has been pushed into the area between the retaining wall and the rear of the hill (Fig. 29). Newspaper is useful for filling such areas as it is cheap, or even free. It is also very lightweight, which is always a bonus when it comes to model landscaping, and, if screwed up tightly enough, it is sufficiently strong to hold the top layer of terrain without sagging. The front of the cutting wall has had

Fig. 28. Retaining walls built in this way are very strong.

Fig. 29. Screwed-up newspaper is used to create the contours of the land.

Fig. 30. The first layers of the hard shell have been added.

a single coat of grey undercoat applied straight from an aerosol tin.

A hard shell was added to the scenery (Fig. 30), using layers of paper coated with diluted PVA glue. (There are other methods of creating hard shells for model landscaping, which will be covered at other points in the book.) To create a hard shell like this one, take a tray or something similar to work in, and dilute some PVA glue approximately 50/50 with water. Cut or tear strips of paper into manageable sizes – the thicker the paper the fewer the number of layers required. Dunk the paper into the diluted PVA or paint the glue on to the paper using a thick decorating brush. Either way, make sure the paper is covered in glue, but not dripping in it. Lay the first sheet of glue-coated paper on to the screwed-up newspaper, then repeat the above process, overlapping the paper strips as you work along. When you have covered the area you are working on, repeat the process, making sure that all the edges and joins are well stuck down. Three layers of paper should be enough for most areas.

Allow the layers to dry out and then give them a couple of coats of neat PVA, allowing the first coat to dry before applying the second. This will result in a hard surface.

The final layer of this hard shell landscaping is a coat of cement mixed with 3 parts water to 1 part PVA (Fig. 31). There are a couple of benefits of using cement: not only does it dry very hard, it also has a good earthy colour when dry and is an excellent base on which to add scenic modelling materials. The mixture is applied with a thick paintbrush and painted all over the surface of the paper. It does not need to be put on too thickly – a thin coating, enough to cover the paper, will suffice.

To achieve the effect of the areas of natural rock on the side of the hill, build up layers of the cement mixture until they are a few millimetres thick. Allow the cement to dry for a while, until it is firm enough

Fig. 31. The final layer of the hard shell has been added.

Tip

It is worth bearing in mind that the layers of rock do not have to be perfectly horizontal. When they are scored at an angle, they give a better impression of naturally occurring seams of rock.

to touch without it moving. Once the cement has started to set, it is hard enough to score without it sagging and therefore closing the score marks up. For this, use a sharp blade and drag it across the surface of the cement to create layers of sedimentary rock. For a more varied effect, use blades of different thickness.

PAINTING AND WEATHERING THE WALL

Earlier in the process of creating the retaining wall, the front was given a coat of grey primer – ordinary auto grey primer is fine. If you are building your cutting walls in situ it is important to ensure that primer does not get all over the track. Before

spraying, cover everything with newspaper and hold it in place using masking tape or similar.

The primer will in this instance serve as the pointing between the courses of stone blocks so make sure that you get good coverage, right into the corners where the pillars meet the wall sections, and underneath the stone plinth, coping and capping stones too. Two lighter coats are preferable to one heavy coat. Ensure the primer is totally dry before continuing with any further application.

MIXING PAINTS

There are so many good-quality paints, pigments and weathering powders available to modellers today for all sorts of effects – stonework included – but the base paint for the stonework on this wall is white matt emulsion. Most people have some somewhere around their house just waiting to be used.

When mixing the paints for the stonework it is advisable to make yourself a palette from which to work. A dinner plate, piece of glossy card or plastic sheet is perfect, as it will not soak up the paint. Place a generous amount of white matt emulsion paint on the palette, then beside it add a few drops of ready-to-use black poster paint and a couple of drops of a yellow poster paint (Ochre Yellow is ideal).

Fig. 32. The undercoated wall is detailed using the dry-brushing method.

The yellow will add slight warmth to the final mix. There is no exact science to the next step, which involves mixing three to four tones of grey, from very dark through to much lighter, adding a touch of yellow to each. It may be a good idea to undercoat a spare sheet of embossed plastic sheet, so that you can practise the next step and see if you have achieved the colours you want. Remember that the paint will dry lighter than it initially goes on, so wait before settling on the specific mix.

DRY BRUSHING

The painting of plastic embossed sheets is easy as long as you follow the basic 'rules'. This is one way to do it.

Take a paintbrush with short, stiff bristles. If necessary, take a trip to your local pound shop and cut the bristles of a cheap brush down. Dip the brush in the paint – not necessarily the tip of the bristles but the side of the brush. Have a clean tissue to hand and wipe most of the paint off the brush, to leave the smallest amount remaining on the bristles. Gently, using the brush side on, rub the bristles over the surface of the raised part of the embossed sheet (Fig. 32).

Although there is not much paint on the brush, it should pick out the stones/bricks perfectly, leaving the undercoated mortar free from any additional paint. You may prefer to give the whole wall a dry brushing of a suitable stone-coloured paint first and then, once it has dried, start dry brushing on a darker paint to represent the weathering and grime that builds up over time. Do not be tempted to pick out individual bricks but work over small areas at a time, changing randomly from the darker tones to the lighter ones. Applying very little paint at each stroke will allow you to control the overall appearance of the wall as you work over it back and forth. The thickness of the emulsion paint stops it leaking into the mortar courses, which is why it is better than other types. It also dries to a very matt finish.

It is worth pointing out that the whole wall can be built away from the layout and fixed in position after the painting process although I always prefer to build features like this in situ wherever possible.

'POINTING'

There are a number of ways to achieve good pointing effects. One is to follow the painting stages in this demonstration, then allow all the coats of paint and weathering powders to dry. When they are perfectly dry, a suitably coloured filler or grab adhesive is worked over the surface of the stonework and into the gaps in between the courses. Not only does this create great-looking mortar, it is also very useful for filling all those tiny gaps you may have around the joins where the various elements of the wall meet. When all the courses have been 'pointed', any excess filler should be removed with a cloth from the face of the bricks.

DETAILING

Further very light coats of dry brushing are added to darken the wall a little more. A subtle layer of weathering was also added, using weathering products from the A K Interactive range of pigments and enamels. The enamels are applied in the same way as the emulsion-based paint, using the dry-brushing method. The pigments introduce some earth tones and warmth to the wall.

Treemendus Scenefix glue is painted between where the track will go and along the base of the wall (Fig. 33). A layer of Earth Powder will be sprin-

Fig. 33. Light weathering adds to the overall effect of the wall.

Fig. 34. The wall is now ready to join the surrounding landscape.

Fig. 35. Work begins on the scenic side of the cutting.

kled over it. The Earth Powder will soak up the glue and set to a very hard finish. To help it soak all the way up through the powder a liberal amount of hairspray is sprayed over the powder. This reacts with the glue and helps it set. It is a good idea to hold a sheet of paper in front of the wall whilst spraying the hairspray as it may leave an unwanted sheen to your newly painted stonework (Fig. 35).

FINISHING TOUCHES

When the layout is finished (Fig. 36), the wall set in the landscape really does appear to be doing the job of holding back the hillside. A layer of Treemendus Spring scatter fine, Mid Summer scatter fine and Earth Powder has been used to cover the cement hard shell. First, a 50/50 mix of water/PVA is painted

Fig. 36. An overall view of the completed cutting.

over the surface, then the scatters are sprinkled directly on to it. To assist it all to stick, a blast of hairspray is applied from about 45cm (18in) once the scatters are in place.

Obviously, a cutting will often require a wall like this on either side of the track as it approaches a tunnel mouth. Once you have mastered the construction of a wall on one side, you can make a mirror image on the other to create such a feature.

There are a number of further modelling stages that may be undertaken in order to complete the diorama. For more details on this groundwork and these scenic additions, see later chapters in the book.

SUMMARY

The main feature of this scene is the cutting wall. There are only three elements that go into making it: wood, card and either embossed plastic sheets or printed paper sheets. It is vital to measure carefully and double check everything before cutting. Stone colour varies enormously from region to region and you should aim to paint your stonework to reflect this.

Fig. 37. A Manchester-bound mixed goods waits for the all-clear to join the mainline. Cutting walls like the one modelled here are abundant throughout the UK. Choosing the correct type of finish for your location will help set the scene.

CHAPTER TWO

NATURAL ROCK CUTTINGS

Fig. 38. A natural rock face in North Yorkshire.

Materials

- Polystyrene sheet (0.5–2in in thickness)
- Cement
- PVA glue
- Paints/weathering powders from A K Interactive
- Water materials from Deluxe Materials
- Static grass from Noch
- Scenic modelling materials from Treemendus
- Hairspray

Tools

- Scalpel/Stanley knife
- Wire
- Selection of paintbrushes
- Scissors
- Noch Gras-Master

As well as the brick-lined cuttings through which your railway might run, there are cuttings that have been blasted through solid rock. The rock is still visible and has become the walls of the cutting, so that there is no need to line it with a retaining wall. With time the rock becomes overgrown and weathered. It is worth noting that some cuttings are a mixture of both natural stone, as in this diorama, and brick or block, as in Chapter 1. It can add interest to your layouts if you use a mixture of both.

Imagine this scene to be a neglected branch line or a track that runs to and from a quarry or a seldom-used yard. Vegetation is taking over and has found pockets of earth and moisture among the cracks and crevices in the cutting wall. Weeds grow alongside the track and amongst the ballast between the sleepers. The principles used here can be used on any overgrown areas of the layout and the effects can make a refreshing contrast with pristinely ballasted track work.

Fig. 39. Track glued in place.

Fig. 40. Basic building materials for the rock face.

PLANNING AND PREPARATION

As with all types of cutting, it is important to leave the correct clearance for all the stock you run, and may run in the future. To ensure that everything will be clear of the tracks, hold a pencil or marker pen to the side of a long-wheel-based carriage and run this around the track. Build the cutting on the opposite side of the line from the track.

There is a difference in the planning between this cutting and the cutting in Chapter 1: whereas the brick-lined cutting is very flat and ordered, this one aims to represent a natural stone wall. One of the features that make these cuttings interesting is that they are not perfectly flat and any protrusions on the wall should ideally be accounted for before fixing in place.

Stone cuttings are, in some ways, easier to build than other types. The top of the cutting will not be capped with stone as it will have grasses and weeds hanging over its edge. As you will be aiming for a much more natural effect, there is also no need to prepare neat wall components from cardboard, with stone sheets glued to it. Polystyrene sheets are ideal as the base for natural stone cuttings and rock faces in general. Polystyrene is very lightweight, easy to break and shape, and will take the cement coating (which is used to create the impression of stone) very well.

To give a little variation in the levels of the terrain, the track is laid on top of a strip of ceiling tile which has been cut to the shape of the cutting you have in mind (Fig. 39). If your track work is already in place, a similar effect can be achieved by removing sections of your baseboard, using a jigsaw or a router, and contouring the recess to suit your individual plan. The sleepers and the rails have been given a coat of matt brown paint. This brown paint will act as an undercoat for the painting and weathering processes that will follow later in the demonstration.

In the example, the track has not been laid in a straight line, because the cutting wall is not as flat as that of a retaining-wall type of cutting. Not only does this add to the realism of the scenery but it can also be a very useful method for taking the trains around a bend between two rock walls and through to a hidden exit into the fiddle yard.

CONSTRUCTION

The materials used to construct rock cuttings should be very lightweight and ideally inexpensive. Here, a mixture of polystyrene sheets, varying in thickness from 1 to 5cm, have been used (Fig. 40). There are other materials that can be used to great effect: for example, cork bark, foam insulation board or even crumpled-up newspaper can provide the frame for

Fig. 41. Making more than you need allows you to play around with the position of the pieces.

Tip

Having far more pieces than you need at this stage gives you the chance to position them in different scenarios. Keep playing around with the position of the pieces until you are happy with the look of the cutting wall. Some natural rock cuttings can be fairly flat. If that is the look you want, position the pieces accordingly. If you want a rugged-looking cutting, place the rocks in a more random fashion. Remember to leave clearance for your stock.

Fig. 42. Position the pieces without glue at first.

a rock face. Cork bark may be painted following the steps below, and fixed in place on the baseboard either before or after the paint is applied. Foam insulation board is harder than polystyrene and can be carved to create very nice-looking rock formations. It can also be coated with the cement mixture (see page 33). Screwed-up newspaper, sealed with PVA, makes a very lightweight option for the shell of a cutting and also takes the cement mixture well.

Sheets of polystyrene can be snapped by hand (Fig. 41). If possible, do this over a bin away from your layout as it can be fairly messy. The snapping results in some random-shaped pieces of material to work with, which for this cutting will be perfect.

Although layers of rock in exposed rock faces are often fairly horizontal, some rock faces are formed from rocks that have been turned and moved until they are almost vertical. In this example, both types of rock will be visible. Placing the polystyrene at a certain angle right at the start of the construction stage can affect the finished result quite dramatically. Once the positioning of the polystyrene has begun (Fig. 42), you can see that to the right-hand side of the cutting there is a horizontal rock face. For the more central section, the base of the polystyrene is cut at an angle to allow it to stand at approximately 60 degrees.

A small amount of PVA, hot glue or grab adhesive can be used to hold the pieces together at this stage (Fig. 43).

Fig. 43. PVA or similar will hold the polystyrene in place.

Fig. 44. Shape the pieces as you build.

Working along the length of the cutting, keep adding polystyrene pieces until you are happy with the basic shape. Edges that appear unrealistic can be snapped off as you work along (Fig. 44). It will also help to stick wire or a cocktail stick through the sheets of polystyrene to hold them in place until the glue dries. Remember not to allow any of the pieces to interfere with the running of the rolling stock; break the protrusions off if necessary. The advantage of using polystyrene is that, as it is so easy to break and carve, any slight modifications that may be needed can be carried out at any time, even after the wall has been coated in its hard shell. However, if you plan correctly there should never be any cause to adjust the rock face after it has been coated.

When creating walls of this nature, you need to avoid leaving a gap between the bottom of the rock face and the baseboard. A gap along the whole length will spoil the look of your cutting, as it will look as though the wall has been placed on top of the board as opposed to sticking up from the earth below it. Certain areas along the wall might look good with a small gap, but do avoid leaving a space along the whole length.

When the whole wall has been constructed (Fig. 45), the gaps between the bottom of the wall and the baseboard can be filled. A small pool of water between the rear of the track and the wall will be used to represent the water that drips from the wall as it works its way through the earth.

In anticipation of the potentially messy coating stage of the wall, the track is masked using masking tape; strips of paper and tape would work equally well. The edges of the ceiling tile to which the track is glued have been shaped to look more natural, and the addition of some rocks in front of the track also gives the impression that this cutting has been cut through rock.

A solid rock arch for the train to go through would be a nice feature, with the added bonus of helping

Fig. 45. Because of its light weight, polystyrene is perfect for this type of construction.

Fig. 46. Wires hold the pieces together whilst the glue dries.

to hide a track that is leaving the layout and joining a fiddle yard. It may be created in the same way as the wall, stacking up polystyrene pieces to clear the trains that run underneath them. The arch is joined to the cutting wall and all is blended together using the methods described below. Arches such as this must appear to be strong and secure as they would have been removed at the time of blasting had they been unsafe.

The hard shell for the ground above the cutting (Fig. 46) can be constructed in a way identical to the stages set out in Chapter 1 (Figs 28–31).

COATING

The board has been cleared of most of the mess; the track is on a higher level than the rest of the baseboard (Fig. 47). A start has been made to fill the gap between the wall and the board; the remainder of the gap will be filled at a later stage using the cement mixture that will be used to coat the polystyrene wall. It is best to fill the larger gaps between the pieces of polystyrene with small bits of polystyrene or screwed-up newspaper, stuck in place with PVA.

The cutting wall will look quite dramatic when it is complete, with the overhanging vertical sandstone providing a striking contrast with the horizontal layers of rock.

To apply the coating, use a half-inch-wide brush (Fig. 48). Load the brush with the mixture and work it into all the little fissures between the polystyrene blocks. If the cement mixture needs thickening at this stage, add more cement. If it needs thinning slightly, add a small amount of water and stir in well. Remember to add the water a few drops at a time. Avoid pulling the brush away from the surface and leaving little hanging points of the mixture as this looks unrealistic. Work

Fig. 47. Dry and ready to coat in the cement mixture.

Fig. 48. Fill all the gaps.

Fig. 49. The rock face blends into the groundwork.

Preparing the coating

To create a realistic and durable surface for the wall you will need to mix together some readily available materials. Some modellers use plaster for this kind of work, but the following combination dries to a very realistic colour even before any paint has even been applied. All the measurements are approximate, but the quantity below will be enough for a cutting approximately 3ft (90cm) in length by 8in (20cm) high.

In a container mix 200ml of PVA glue and 400ml of clean cold water, to form a milky liquid, then add two mugs full of ordinary household cement and a half mug of Treemendus Earth Powder. Blend the liquid and powder together to form a thick creamy paste. Add more water or cement as necessary. The PVA will keep the mixture workable for quite a while but if you need to freshen it up, add a drop of washing-up liquid and give it a stir.

ADDING MORE DETAIL

Any little imperfections can be brushed away whilst the cement is still wet (Fig. 50), then it is a good idea to give the whole wall a closer inspection to make sure that all the original surface has been covered and there are no white areas showing through the cement. More detail can also be added at this stage. To create an area that appears to be water-worn, build up a thick layer and then carve a groove out from the rock face whilst the cement is partly set.

After you have added in all the detail, the protective tape can be removed from the track, revealing the scale of the rock face (Fig. 51). There are various methods of adding texture to the rock but it should be allowed to dry for an hour or so before any further work is carried out. To achieve thin layers of sedimentary rock, the semi-dry cement can be worked on with a few wires that have been twisted together to form a 'fork' with about ten 'prongs'. This is carefully dragged horizontally along the face of the cutting wall to produce thin 'layers' in the rock

over the entire area, making sure to cover all the exposed polystyrene. Paint the mixture on thicker in some places and thinner in others, so as to leave the texture of the polystyrene just visible on the cutting surface. Keep applying the mixture until the whole area has been coated (Fig. 49).

When adding the coating, apply the brush strokes in the direction in which the polystyrene is lying – horizontal strokes for horizontal pieces and vertical strokes for pieces that are standing upright. (Note that, at this stage, the hard shell has been added to the paper above the rock face and to the ground around the track.)

Fig. 50. Detail can be added using a paintbrush and wires. Large gaps can be filled in at this stage too.

Fig. 51. Removing the protective tape.

face. Alternatively, use a few cocktail sticks taped together for the process.

In the example, some of the rock face has been given a different treatment, being smoothed over with a paintbrush and given a sprinkling of Earth Powder. This will give certain areas of the wall a very different look from the rest, giving the impression of different types of stone making up the geology of

the area. Later in the weathering process the rocks will be weathered using the same materials and blend together perfectly but still retain the look of different kinds of rock.

After the texture has been added and allowed to dry (Fig. 52), the coating should be very hard and durable whilst still remaining very light in weight. There is already a noticeable difference in the colour

Fig. 52. The rock face was allowed two days to dry.

Fig. 53. A dark wash being added.

PAINTING

To add more detail to the cutting wall it is necessary to give it a few coats of paint. The colour wash applied to the example (Fig. 53) is a black poster paint with a tiny bit of white poster paint added and diluted by approximately 6 parts water to 1 part paint. Diluted acrylic paints may also be used at this stage; they are used later in the weathering process too. There is no specific way to apply the paint and a random covering often works better than a more methodical approach. This application of dark paint is in order to darken all the cracks and crevices in the wall, so do not be alarmed if your wall overall looks too dark at this stage. As the cement soaks up the paint and as the paint dries the surface of the wall will lighten. This is then dry brushed with various shades of paint to pick out all the tiny details in the cement and add to the effect of a natural stone cutting.

and texture of the various types of rock. Note also that, although the layers in the rock are horizontal, they need not be perfectly horizontal. The effect of the Earth's crust moving around over millions of years can be achieved by dragging the wires at a slight angle to the horizontal.

Once the initial dark wash has dried, the lighter shades can be dry brushed on (Fig. 54), as with the wall in Chapter 1. Apply the paint in vertical strokes so as not to get paint in the cracks and crevices. Matt white emulsion may be used as the main paint for

Fig. 54. Mid-tones being added.

Fig. 55. Highlights being added.

Fig. 56. Shade being added.

the mixes; to give variety in the appearance of your wall, try three different shades based on the same paint colours:

- Mix 1: 8 parts matt white; 3 parts yellow; 2 parts black.
- Mix 2: 8 parts matt white; 2 parts yellow; 1 part black.
- Mix 3: 10 parts matt white; 1 part yellow; 0.5 part black.

These mixes are by no means rigid, but they show that, by mixing three or more different shades of a similar colour, you can achieve a realistic effect with some subtle variety. The different tones of paint add to the light and shade effect on the wall, and they are also guaranteed to blend together well.

The process is best done in layers. Dry brush the whole wall with the darker shade of paint, using vertical strokes, then start again using a lighter shade. As you work along the wall you can add tiny spots of brown emulsion paint to vary the colour.

When applying the lightest shade of paint, use downward strokes only. This gives the impression of weather-worn rock on the edges of wall where it has been bleached by the effects of the sun (Fig. 55). Avoid using pure black or white as these colours can

look unrealistic. The example is styled and painted to represent limestone with a couple of areas of sandstone. If you want a faithful representation of the area you are modelling remember that field trips or searching online are the best way to collect the relevant information.

Shading the undersides of any overhangs using dark paint in upward strokes is also an effective way of introducing shadows to the wall (Fig. 56).

It might be wise to paint a test piece first and leave it to dry, to see if the end result will be the colour of rock you want to achieve.

GROUNDWORK

The first layer of groundwork is added to the foot of the cutting and around the trackside (Fig. 57). Whilst the Earth Powder is being added to the groundwork, a small amount is brushed on to the lower parts of the cutting wall. This is the first step in weathering the wall and will also help it to blend visually into the rest of the groundwork. Note how the track is already becoming part of the scenery.

Weathering pigments and enamel paints from A K Interactive, realistic water modelling materials from Deluxe Materials, static grass fibres from Noch and scenic modelling materials from Treemendus will

Fig. 57. Weathering the rock will blend it in with the groundwork.

Fig. 58. Some of the materials used to detail the wall.

be used to weather and blend the hillside, wall and trackside groundwork together (Fig. 58).

AK Interactive Fresh Mud Enamel, Earth Effects Enamel, Slimy Grime Light and Dark Enamels and European Earth and Dark Earth pigments have all been used to weather this scene. Also added to give further colour and texture to the wall are some scatters from Treemendus. Fine Spring, Mid Summer and Late Summer scatters have been fixed

to the wall using Scenefix glue. Diluted PVA glue (3 parts water to 1 part glue) can also be used to hold the scatters. A little Earth Powder has also been sprinkled on to the glue holding the scatters in place.

Treemendus Limestone Scree has been added to the groundwork around the track and at the bottom of the wall. Note that this is the same colour as the rock in the wall and looks as though it has fallen from

Fig. 59. Early stages of weathering.

Fig. 60. A trickle of water feeds the trackside pool – this will dry clear.

the hillside naturally. Often, the best way to add the smaller fallen rocks to a landscape is simply to throw them on to the baseboard and fix them where they land (Fig. 59).

When the groundwork has dried, a small water feature is added between the track and the wall, along with evidence on the wall showing where the water runs down towards the pool. Deluxe Materials Solid Water, a two-part resin, is mixed according to the instructions and added to the landscape using the syringe supplied. The water is allowed to find its own level and forms a shallow pool beside the track. This pool used 10ml of resin. A trickle of water is added coming down the wall, using Deluxe Materials Making Waves product, which dries clear, and it is this that appears to be feeding the pool (Fig. 60).

Further detail is added to the groundwork using Treemendus Raw Grass, a teddy-bear fur fabric that is an excellent choice for adding dry or dead grasses to your layouts (Fig.61). Using a pair of sharp

Fig. 61. Raw Grass before it has been trimmed from its backing sheet. The sheet on the right has been lightly coloured using diluted Sap Green acrylic paint.

Fig. 62. Raw Grass trimmed into tiny fibres with scissors.

Fig. 63. Raw Grass tufts being glued to the cutting wall.

scissors, trim some of the fibres off the sheet. The fibres are about 1in (2.5cm) in length, but for the effect desired here they should be trimmed into tiny pieces (Fig. 62). Take time to trim them really small – they should end up resembling coloured fluff.

Distribute the trimmed fibres along the hillside around the track and on the cutting wall, and work them into the groundwork using a thin wooden stick and your finger (Fig. 63). A generous misting of

hairspray will hold them in place. Use diluted PVA to fix the tufts to the walls, pushing them into the glue with a sharp stick. This time, leave the fibres standing upright to represent tall weeds growing on the face of the cutting.

Now that all the components of the scene are really starting to blend together (Fig. 64), the rails can be given a coat of AK Interactive track rust pigment. They will be toned down later in the weathering process. More scatters and Earth Powder are added to the front of the scene and these will serve as a base on which to fix Noch static grass fibres.

To add to the overgrown look of the cutting, some small shrubs and bushes can be planted on and around the cutting wall (Fig. 65). These shrubs are really very easy to make, using synthetic hair for the structure combined with scenic scatters for the foliage. For more detail on making shrubs, *see* Chapters 3, 6, 7, 9 and 10.

In order to fix the shrubs to the groundwork and cutting wall, neat PVA glue is applied with a small paintbrush to the area where the shrub is required. In the real world, a railway cutting such as this can easily gather enough organic material in fissures and crevices to allow plants and weeds to root and take hold. Push the shrubs into the glue with a wooden skewer,

Fig. 64. A general view of the cutting so far.

Fig. 65. Shrubs ready to be 'planted' in the landscape.

toothpick or something similar (Fig. 66). The amount of growth you add to your cutting wall will depend on the look you would like to create. Overcrowding the wall with too many plants can detract from the wall itself; however, if the cutting is to be used as a scenic break, then extra growth may help to hide the point at which the trains exit. Avoid positioning the shrubs too uniformly as this will make the whole scene look man-made and not natural at all.

To add to the overgrown look of the scene, Noch static grass fibres are added using a Noch Gras-Master static grass applicator. The quality of the grasses, tufts and weeds produced using this applicator is excellent. To 'plant' the grass a thin

Fig. 66. Gluing shrubs to the base.

Fig. 67. Preparing the groundwork for static grass.

Tip

It is best to start with shorter, brighter-coloured fibres and add longer fibres of differing colours to achieve the best results, as this gives some variety to the overall look of the grass. If fibres of only one length are used, you may end up with a manicured 'lawn' effect.

Fig. 68. Applying the first blend of static grass fibres.

layer of Noch grass glue is painted over the area to be covered (Fig. 67).

The Noch Gras-Master uses static electricity to charge fibres which are placed in its hopper. A small crocodile clip attaches to the track, or to a pin inserted into the baseboard, close to where the grass is to be added. These fibres, when shaken over the glue, leave the applicator in an upright position and stick in the glue to produce a very realistic grass effect (Fig. 68).

Whilst the glue is still wet, a second, longer fibre is added to give variety to the grass. To finish, a light dusting of Treemendus Earth Powder is sprinkled over the grass patch. This will stick to the glue beneath it. The Earth Powder will blend all the fibres together and take the shine off the glue, which otherwise may remain visible once it has dried, especially if PVA is used.

THE COMPLETED DIORAMA

There are masses of interesting points to consider in the final diorama (Fig. 69). It could be even further enhanced with a gang of figures working along the

Fig. 69. A realistic cutting that is full of character.

line, perhaps, or a small platelayer's hut or log pile as a focal point. Old fencing with brambles growing through it along the top of the cutting would be a good addition to the scene, and trees could also be added to introduce more natural features. There are many possibilities and the list goes on ...

SUMMARY

Like the cutting in Chapter 1, this one would have been cut out of the landscape and the track would be running between two cutting walls. The same principles apply to both versions.

This cutting was styled on a rock face in Ingleton in the Yorkshire Dales National Park (Fig. 38). Rock varies enormously from region to region and it is advisable either to visit or refer to photographs before embarking on the project. Readily available materials in the form of polystyrene and cement are the two main constituents of the cutting wall – always double check that the correct clearance has been left between the wall and rolling stock before detailing it. Dry brushing is an easy and effective way to bring out the texture of the rock face and will highlight all the little fissures as you progress through the various steps.

Fig. 70. Pannier tank 5764 hauls a single 'Crocodile H' well wagon through the cutting. Note the subtle difference in the types of rocks modelled in the cutting wall.

CHAPTER THREE

GRASSY HILLSIDES

Fig. 71. In nature, grasses can grow to a surprising height.

Materials

- Timber
- Chicken wire
- Scenery Maker (plaster-impregnated cloth)
- PVA glue
- Raw Grass (teddy-bear fur fabric)
- Scenic modelling materials
- Paints/weathering powders

Tools

- Scalpel/Stanley knife
- Wire cutters
- Stapler
- Scissors
- Bucket
- Assorted paintbrushes

A hill is an area of land that is higher than the land surrounding it. Hillsides, often covered in grass, are a frequent feature of the countryside that is seen from the window of a train. A hillside is the sloping side of a hill before it reaches its flatter top. Using a range of materials, it is possible to create a gently sloping late-summer grassy hillside, and thus produce a very realistic-looking landscape. Many of the techniques used to create grassy hillsides can also be used to create embankments on model railways.

In the past, the embankments alongside railways had to be kept free from plants and weeds because of the risk of fire from the coal-fuelled engines. Today, the fuels used in the UK are much less likely to cause fire as the trains travel down the tracks, so the hillsides and embankments often feature many types of greenery. This gives the modeller plenty of opportunity to incorporate plants and weeds when creating the trackside environment.

If you decide to represent an actual landscape, study photographs or plan a field trip to see what it looks like. Hills range in appearance from very gentle and rolling to very tall and steep. They may be divided into individual fields by walls, fences, hedges or rows of trees. Neighbouring fields can look very different; some may be completely covered with trees and foliage whilst others will be well grazed and kept free from most growth.

During the summertime sheep may be seen in large flocks grazing on the lush grass the hills provide. There is a huge variety in the colour and texture of the plants and grasses that make up a hillside's surface. Depending on the time of year, the colours can range from pale straw to bright greens through to dark green, and there are also a wide range of textures, provided by heathers, wild flowers, ferns, reeds and weeds.

PLANNING

Hills on model railways add not only height but can also add dramatic features to the layout. On an end-to-end layout, a hillside can stretch all the way across the rear of the scene taking the eye up towards the back and to any features on the horizon. A cutting leading to a tunnel mouth at the edge of an end-to-end layout can be used to great effect to disguise the fact that trains are leaving the scenic part of the layout.

When incorporated into a continuous layout, a hillside can be used to break up the track and help to hide the fact the trains are going round and round. This is especially effective if the train can be stopped on a storage line out of sight of the viewer for a while, emerging later as if returning from a distant destination.

BEGINNING CONSTRUCTION

Chicken wire is used to create the basic shape of the hillside. Staple the edge of the chicken wire directly to the baseboard and gently bend and twist it until the desired shape of the landscape is achieved. Timber supports, cut to length and fixed vertically to the baseboard using either PVA glue or held in place with screws from underneath, will help the chicken wire to stay in place. Using both PVA and screws will be more secure. The supports hold the chicken-

wire frame in position and also stop the structure from sagging as the scenic steps are undertaken. It is recommended that you staple the wire to the top of the supports too.

Another way of creating the basic shape of the landscape involves using sheets of polystyrene or foam, which are glued in place horizontally and carved to create natural-looking undulations. Card formers and screwed-up newspaper supporting sheets of paper soaked with diluted PVA glue can also be useful for making strong, lightweight scenic features.

The first step in creating the hillside in the example is to add some vertical timber supports to the baseboard (Fig. 72). You will need to plan ahead with these, as they will govern how steep and how high your hillside will be when it is covered with scenic materials. Try to add some variety to the height of each support but also allow the hillside to flow naturally. This hillside will rise gently so short supports are added towards the front of the hill with taller supports being added towards the back. Saw off the top of each support at an angle to mirror the gradient of the slope. This will allow the chicken wire to pass naturally over the supports without creating flat spots when securing with staples.

Start by drilling a small hole through the baseboard where each of the supports is to be positioned, then drill a pilot hole into one end of each of the

Fig. 72. The timber supports glued and screwed in position.

Fig. 73. Chicken wire is added to create the contours.

Fig. 74. Scenery Maker is applied – note the overlaps.

supports and fix them in place from below using screws. A spot of PVA glue will help to hold the supports firmly.

Once the supports are fixed in place and the glue has been allowed to dry, the chicken wire can be added. Even bare chicken wire can transform an empty board into a landscape with character. The front edge of the chicken wire can be fixed in place to the baseboard using staples – a heavy-duty staple gun is required for most baseboard material and is well worth investing in. Carefully shape the wire to give a realistic-looking terrain. For this gently rolling hillside there is no need for any major lumps or bumps. Staple the wire to the tops of the supporting timber posts as you work along your layout (Fig. 73).

It is advisable to drill a series of holes or even cut away a section of board beneath the chicken wire to allow air to circulate. This will ensure that the plaster-coated bandage will dry out completely. Scenery Maker (a plaster-covered cloth by Javis) is used to cover the chicken wire and give a firm base on which to add the scenic detail. It sets very hard and is a most durable way to create model landscape shells.

When adding Scenery Maker to the chicken-wire contours, it is best to cut all the pieces required to fit the area you are about to cover before you start to apply it, and have them to hand as you work. Cut enough to allow for three or four layers and account

for a little overlap too when cutting the pieces (Fig. 74). To activate the plaster, simply dampen the bandage with cold water (avoid over-wetting it) and place it on to the chicken wire. Laying the layers in different directions will make for a stronger landscape. Scenery Maker will set within twenty-four hours under normal conditions and will produce a very solid foundation on which to build.

CREATING GRASS

Whilst the hard landscaping is drying, you can make a start on the grass that will cover the hillside.

There are many materials available for creating model grass, from ready-to-use grass mats to scatters, static grasses and fur fabrics. In the example, a mixture of all these materials is used, but the main component is Raw Grass (teddy-bear fur fabric). This provides a very versatile way to create grass, as it can be coloured to match a specific scheme and trimmed to the required length. There are many different effects that can be achieved easily using this material.

CUTTING AND TRIMMING

The fibres on the Raw Grass sheet are approximately 1in (2.5cm) in length, which equates to around 6ft (180cm) in 1:76 scale. Now, although grass does not grow to this height, clumps of grasses, brambles, nettles and other common weeds can stand 5–6ft (150–180cm) tall, so some of the fibres may be left in small clumps without any trimming at all. This will add to the variety of the hillside's appearance. The majority of the fibres on the sheet will be trimmed to just a fraction of an inch (3–4mm) in length.

Use a sheet of fabric large enough to cover the area you are detailing. Cut it to shape by laying it over the chicken-wire landscape, leaving a small overhang, which will be trimmed off once the grass is glued in place. If it is necessary to use two or more sheets, the joins can be hidden without trace if a little care is taken.

Fig. 75. Initial trimming of the Raw Grass.

Trim the fibres to a suitable length using scissors (Fig. 75); hair clippers can be used but this tends to give a more manicured effect. The first step in creating realistic grass is to comb the fibres so that they stand more or less upright. Take a pair of sharp scissors and trim in random directions, to avoid creating 'tramlines' in your hillside. This is quite a time-consuming job but worth persevering with as the results can be stunning. Remember to leave certain areas with longer fibres, to be turned into patches of weeds and brambles later. Try to avoid cutting too close to the backing sheet as it may show through the fibres. If it does show through, it can be covered up in the later steps.

Do not throw the trimmings away (Fig. 76), but store them in a re-sealable bag or container with a lid. They will be used all over your model railway when you come to adding the scenery. They can be used to fill joins where two pieces of fabric are butted up together, to hide small gaps between walls and other features and the baseboard, and to add colour and texture to all the groundwork, including the hillside. The leftover fibres may also be used to hide the edges of the fabric where it joins other elements of the groundwork.

When the trimming has been completed, take the sheet outside and give it a good shake. This will remove all the tiny fibres which will be present and help separate the longer fibres (Fig. 77).

Fig. 76. Keep the offcuts for a later use.

Fig. 77. Trimmed sheet with all the loose fibres removed.

Fig. 78. Brushed and ready for painting.

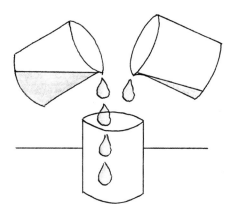

Fig. 79. Diluted Sap Green acrylic paint.

Take a comb or brush and thoroughly comb through the fibres so they are all lying in the same direction (Fig. 78). Take the sheet outside again and, with the fibres facing you, give it a sharp shake, to help separate the fibres again and force them to stand upright.

COLOURING

Choose a base paint colour for the grass – Sap Green acrylic, used here, is a good base colour, but you are free to choose whatever you prefer. Pre-diluted poster paint can also be used. The Sap Green paint is diluted at a ratio of 4 parts water to 1 part paint (Fig. 79). Again, this is open to experiment and you can dilute your paint to suit your own personal requirements. Sometimes as much as 8 parts water (or more) to 1 part paint may be used, to give a very pale tone to the fabric. If possible, test your mix on an off-cut.

The diluted paint is applied to the sheet in the form of drops. An atomizer type of bottle can be used if preferred, with the paint being sprayed on in a fine mist. It is important not to over-wet the fabric as a little paint will go a long way. Rub the paint through the fibres with your hand, making sure to work it down into the long fibres too.

Comb the fabric again while the paint is still wet, to help disperse the paint through the fibres even more. The sheet should now be left to dry (Fig. 80).

Trimming a path through the fabric will add even more character to the hillside. This will be detailed once the grass is in place on the chicken-wire frame. Paths like this often take the shortest route from

---

Tip

As you apply the paint to the fabric, remember that hillsides are rarely a single tone of green so try to vary the density of the tones of your grass as you work along.

Fig. 80. The first coat of paint has been applied.

one place to another and, like train tracks, have to go around or through natural obstacles in the landscape.

APPLYING THE GRASS

When the Raw Grass sheet has dried it can be stuck to the chicken-wire shell, which has been prepared. Take a large paintbrush and apply a thin layer of PVA glue diluted with water (1 PVA/1 water) to the surface of the Scenery Maker. Starting at the foot of the hill (Fig. 81), fix the fabric to the chicken-wire structure, making sure it is firmly pressed into the glue. When the glue has dried the overhang of fabric can be trimmed off. If required, the edges can be given a further coat of glue to keep them in place.

Fig. 81. Diluted PVA glue holds the fabric to the landscape.

DETAILING

At this stage, you can start to transform the Raw Grass sheet from its current form into something that really resembles a lush hillside. Use the comb to brush all the long fibres so that they are standing upright. Take a firm paintbrush (Fig. 82) and dry brush some neat Sap Green acrylic paint on to the long fibres – do not use too much, but just enough to make them stand out from the rest of the grass. Most of the dry-brushed Sap Green paint will actually be covered as you progress through the next steps, but any fibres that do show through will add an extra subtle tone to the groundwork.

To add another visual element to the hillside, Earth Powder has been added to the groundwork between some of the areas of short grass (Fig. 83). These areas will be enhanced with more scenic materials during the process of detailing the hillside. Earth Powder is particularly useful for hiding any backing sheet that may be showing through the grass.

Invariably when using Raw Grass material to create grass there will be places where the edge of the fabric needs to be blended into the surrounding groundwork (Fig. 84). This edge at the bottom of the hill would be facing the viewer and must be disguised. Take a large handful of the fibres that were cut off the sheet during the preparation of the grass. Split the fibres into three or four separate piles. One pile will retain its natural colour. The other three will be coloured using diluted Sap Green paint, with a slight

Fig. 82. Enhancing the hillside.

Fig. 83. Earth Powder adds more realism to the scene.

Fig. 84. Exposed edges can be hidden seamlessly.

Fig. 85. Loose fibres are painted and left to dry.

difference in tone between the piles. There is no need to over-wet the fibres (Fig. 85). Set aside to dry.

When the paint has dried it is time to trim each pile into very, very fine fibres. The finer you chop the fibres, the better the result will be. Start chopping the first pile over a sheet of card or newspaper. When all the fibres have been trimmed, pick them up off the card and trim them again. Repeat this process until you cannot possibly trim them further. Brush all the fibres into a pile on the card and repeat the process with the other three piles. You will end up with three or four piles of very finely chopped fibres, each in a slightly different tone (Fig. 86). These tiny

pieces will be used to hide any edges of fabric and to detail the grass on the hillside.

Take some diluted PVA (3 parts water to 1 part PVA) and apply it liberally with a small paintbrush to the area where the edge of the fabric joins the groundwork. Pinch small amounts of fibres from the finely chopped piles and place them along the length of the fabric's edge. Using a wooden skewer or something similar, work the fibres into the glue, at the same time making sure that the edge of the fabric is being hidden (Fig. 87). Tiny pinches of Earth Powder or fine scatter can be added on top of the wet glue to add more realism and help disguise the

Fig. 86. The finely chopped fibres are ready for use.

Fig. 87. The chopped fibres easily hide the exposed edges.

Fig. 88. Adding detail to the grassy hillside. The effect is much more convincing once the glue dries.

Fig. 89. Fibres added along the path start to highlight the feature, giving it more character.

edge of the fabric. A hedge or fence could be placed along the bottom of the hill to hide the edge but there may still be areas where this method is required to hide small areas of exposed backing sheet.

The same steps should be followed when disguising the tiny gap left where two pieces of fabric have been joined.

PVA glue, diluted to a ratio of 3 parts water to I part glue, is added carefully along the area that has been trimmed very short to give the impression of a path running across the corner of the hill. Earth Powder is sprinkled over the wet glue (Fig. 88). The Earth Powder soaks up the glue and when dry will give a very pleasing, realistic-looking path. A spray of hairspray will help the surface of the path to set solid.

Using the same fibres that serve to hide the edge of the fabric at the bottom of the hill, more detail can be added on the hillside itself. Using a paintbrush, paint some diluted PVA along the edge of the path and slightly beyond the border of the path into the grass either side of it. Use a wooden skewer to work the palest fibres into areas where you would expect to see dead grass. In the example, the edges of the path are given a dressing of the fibres (Fig. 89). These fibres are also very useful for covering areas where you may have trimmed too short and exposed the backing sheet. When you are happy with the look

of your hillside, give the whole area a spray with hairspray.

While the hillside is still wet (Fig. 90) the areas of pale grass will look quite bright, but they will blend in more naturally once the glue has dried. Fibres can then be added or removed as desired, and after this the next stage of detailing can be undertaken. The overall effect is achieved by introducing more materials with different colours, textures and densities. Scatters, static grass, rubberized horsehair, Raw Grass, Seamoss, and laser-cut paper plants will all

Fig. 90. Leave the groundwork to dry before adding any more detail.

help to bring some of the more overgrown areas to life.

The first step in detailing the patches of Raw Grass that have purposely been left longer than the majority of the hillside is to cover them with scenic glue. Hairspray will work well for this step but if you apply scenic glue to the grass using a firm-bristled brush it is easier to control where it settles. Apply the glue to the areas you want to cover with scatter, making sure the consistency is not too thick (Fig. 91). Sprinkle a small amount of Treemendus fine Mid Summer scatter and fine Spring scatter over the glue and use a wooden skewer, cocktail stick or something similar to stand the grass upright and separate the fibres (Fig. 92). This will stop the grass from drying too clumpy.

The area is then sprayed with a little more scenic glue and given another application of the same scatters used in the previous step (Fig. 93). A small pinch of Earth Powder is also added, to give a slight variation in the tones of the clump. The grass at the top of the hill and to the right-hand side of the path is detailed in the same way. The glue on the groundwork will show while it is still wet, but it will be invisible once it has been allowed to dry.

In the example (Fig. 94), scenic glue was painted on to some sections along the path and again sprayed on to the long grass patches, and static grass fibres are added to the glue. The aim here was not to add too many fibres – just enough to give the impression

Tip

There is a logical order in which to detail the hillside. It is best to start with the finer scatters and static grass first, to give some tonal and textural variety to certain areas of the hillside. You can then add individual details such as brambles, tufts, reeds, shrubs and plants. Working in this order prevents everything getting covered in scatter and static grass fibres. The main aim, though, is to create a realistic scene, so some blending of materials is acceptable, as this will give a more natural effect.

Fig. 91. Glue being applied to the long tufts of Raw Grass.

Fig. 92. A layer of fine scatter is applied to the tufts which are teased into place with a wooden skewer.

Fig. 93. Scatter is applied to all the long tufts in one session, giving a consistency to the groundwork.

Fig. 94. Short static grass is applied over the scatter.

Fig. 95. Long static grass fibres are pushed into the tufts by hand.

of long grass that had started to die back and had mostly fallen to the ground.

To further enhance the landscape, Noch static grass fibres were added to the bottom of the hillside and long static grass fibres were pushed into the patches of scatter-covered Raw Grass by hand. When adding fibres by hand, pinch a small amount between your forefinger and thumb and dip one end of them into neat glue. To improve the look of the groundwork even further, long fibres of unpainted Raw Grass were added to the scatter-covered patches, to create a nice blend of colours and textures (Fig. 95). To add the unpainted Raw Grass tufts, trim a few fibres from the backing sheet, again holding them between forefinger and thumb, and cut their ends using scissors. This creates a flat end, which is carefully dipped into neat PVA glue and then worked into the scatter-covered grass. Subtlety is the name of the game here – add just enough tufts to give some variety to the landscape. A light misting of hairspray will help hold them in place.

Brambles often grow on hillsides and around the perimeter of fields and meadows, and these can be produced easily by using rubberized horsehair. The horsehair is teased out by pulling at it with both hands. Once the right density has been achieved it can be sprayed with a suitable paint – dark brown or black work well, but red may also be suitable,

depending on the time of year depicted. Spray the painted horsehair, wet or dry, with a liberal amount of hairspray, then, while the hairspray is still wet, sprinkle the whole form with a suitable scatter, such as Mid Summer medium (Fig. 96). The next step involves spraying it again, either with scenic glue or dilute PVA (3 parts water to 1 part glue). Leave it to dry for twenty-four hours or so, after which it will be ready to use.

Brambles can spread over a huge area if left unchecked but in this example they are used sparingly. Taking a pair of scissors, trim some of the

Fig. 96. Rubberized horsehair makes very convincing brambles.

Fig. 97. Small clumps of brambles are added to the hillside.

Fig. 98. Dead reeds are added poking through the brambles.

horsehair, to leave a piece that is flat on one side. Apply some PVA to the flat side, or to the groundwork where you want to fix it, and push it into place. It is important to blend it with the rest of the groundwork, so that it does not look as though it has simply been placed on top of it (Fig. 97). You can improve the blending by using some of the Raw Grass fibres that you prepared earlier to hide the edge of the backing sheet.

Three clumps of dead reeds were added to the groundwork to provide the scene with another colour and texture (Fig. 98). Once the glue has dried

the whole hillside can be vacuumed, to remove any loose scatter and static grass fibres.

Even at this stage of detailing you can see how easy it is to create groundwork. To add yet another element to the hillside, you can make a few small dense bushes with Seamoss, a natural product that lends itself well to the creation of small trees and shrubs. It is generally sold in its natural colour, which is yellowish or even reddish. To get the best from Seamoss, it is advisable to spray it a suitable bark colour before applying scatter. For dense bushes, snap small pieces of the plant off and squeeze them

Fig. 99. Seamoss shrubs are added to the top of the hillside.

Fig. 100. A general view of the groundwork, which will be tidied up once all the materials are fixed in position.

Fig. 101. A few laser-cut plants add to the realism of the scene.

together to create one small canopy. This is then dipped in dilute PVA and sprinkled with a suitable scatter to suit the season being modelled. The 'trunk' is then dipped in neat PVA and the shrub is simply set in position on the hillside. Generally, less is more with any of the steps here – a few well-placed shrubs will add more character than a field full (Fig. 99). It is worth noting that, as with real garden design, planting or positioning features in triangular arrangements and using odd numbers tends to work better.

Fig. 102. The completed scene, with a Land Rover and hut helping to bring the hillside to life.

THE COMPLETED DIORAMA

A few laser-cut plants from Noch add even more realistic detail to the groundwork and a hand-made tree stands sentry at the entrance to the field. It appears to be a huge tree in the distance but in reality stands only 5in (12.5cm) tall and adds some perspective to the overall scene. A Land Rover has just been driven over the brow of the hill and shows the scale of the grass and foliage to great effect, as does the small shed. Figures, animals or a tractor going about its business would also add perspective.

SUMMARY

By following a few simple steps, a scene full of late-summer character can be created. Natural daylight really helps to bring out the colours in the finished diorama. Careful application of paint and scenic materials will help you to reproduce the many different tones of green that are seen in nature, creating a realistic interpretation. All the different materials blend together and appear to be growing naturally, without any obvious sign that they have been layered on top of each other.

By using a Raw Grass sheet and only a handful of scenic modelling materials, a grassy hillside is a fairly straightforward project, transforming bare chicken-wire foundations into something of great beauty and charm. It does help to have an image in your mind of the result you would like to achieve, and photographs of the real landscape will be a great source of reference. For many of the elements modelled in the above steps, you can also refer to Chapter 2.

Fig. 103. Two InterCity 125 units pass each other at speed on the East Coast mainline. Longer grass in the foreground and shorter grass to the rear of the scene add to the perspective of the scene, which has been created on only a very narrow baseboard.

CHAPTER FOUR

ROCKY HILLSIDES

Fig. 104. A natural rocky outcrop in Derbyshire.

Materials

- Corrugated cardboard
- Kingspan/polystyrene sheets
- Newspaper
- PVA glue
- Finishing plaster
- Brown/green emulsion paint
- Scenic modelling materials
- Treemendus tree kit
- Paints/weathering powders

Tools

- Steel rule
- Scalpel/Stanley knife
- Large paintbrush
- Spatula/butter knife
- Small chisel
- Static grass applicator

While some hillsides roll gently across the landscape, others are more rugged, with an abundance of rocky outcrops, worn areas of grass and evidence of mini landslides showing the earth and rocks that lie just below the surface. Such hillsides are often criss-crossed by mile upon miles of characteristic drystone walls.

PREPARATION

Polystyrene, Styrofoam, chicken wire, cardboard and paper are all suitable lightweight materials for creating the terrain on which to build hillsides. In the example, thick corrugated cardboard formers have been used to give the hillside its shape. Ply board, polystyrene sheet, or similar lightweight sheet materials can also be used to create the formers; the gaps between the formers will then be filled in with screwed-up newspaper. Rocky outcrops will be fashioned from Kingspan, a rigid polyurethane foam sheet used as insulation in the building trade.

The first step is to style the formers, using thick corrugated cardboard. The cardboard needs to be bigger than the overall dimensions of the hillside, to allow for trimming to shape, and should have a ninety-degree angle to one corner. This corner will be positioned to the back of the layout, with one of the straight edges being fixed to the horizontal baseboard; the other will be vertical, becoming the back of the hill.

The space available on your baseboard will govern the area your hillside covers, but, within reason, it may be as tall as you want. The projected shape of the hillside is drawn on to the cardboard formers, which are then trimmed with a sharp blade to give a natural-looking outline (Fig. 105). These formers will eventually be holding up the ground level of the hillside so, if height is an issue, especially when storing or transporting the layout, it is important to allow for the rocky outcrops, which will be added later and will give additional height.

Once the formers are in position on the baseboard (Fig. 106), small lengths of cardboard are glued either side of them to hold them in place. Small blocks of timber could also be used for this purpose. In addition to the vertical formers, horizontal pieces of cardboard are glued across them, not only to strengthen the framework but also to act as a bed on which to glue the rocky outcrops and drystone wall. Make sure these are slightly lower

than the eventual level of the groundwork. Leave the structure to dry before doing any more work on it.

While the framework of the hillside is drying, prepare the Kingspan, which will become the base for the rocky outcrops that will be protruding from the hillside. Allow more depth to the outcrops than you actually want to see above ground level. This allows them to be buried into the groundwork rather than just being placed on top of it and will result in a much more realistic model (Fig. 107).

SHAPING

The outcrops are carved from the Kingspan, using a sharp knife to fashion the shape of the stone, and to cut vertical and horizontal grooves. At this stage not too much detail is required, as the surface will be coated in a thin layer of finishing plaster, which will then be carved using a sharp chisel to resemble the rock more closely. Follow the mixing instructions on the finishing plaster, mixing enough to cover the Kingspan with a 2–3mm layer. Apply the plaster using a small spatula or butter knife (Fig. 108). As you apply the plaster, you can create layers and small ledges of rock, although these need not be too precise as further details will be carved once the plaster has dried. Allow the plaster to dry completely.

Any remaining plaster can be spread on a thin sheet of plastic or a plastic bag in varying thicknesses,

Fig. 105. Measure and trim all the elements needed to build the framework.

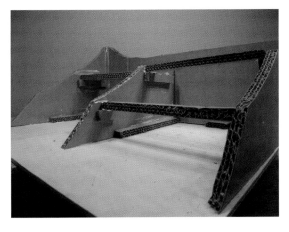

Fig. 106. The framework should be left to dry before the next step.

Fig. 107. Shaping the Kingspan outcrops.

Fig. 108. Plaster is applied to the Kingspan.

and left to dry out. This will be used later as the bits of stone that have fallen from the main rock face.

Once the outcrops are almost dry they can be carved to give the characteristics of the rock; in the example it is sandstone. The outcrops may be carved in situ, but it is best to carve them away from the layout as this keeps the dust away from your track work. Use a sharp craft knife or small chisel to shape the plaster. At this point brush over the surface of the rock with a toothbrush, to remove any bits that have come loose during the carving and to take some of the sharpness from the edges of the

rock (Fig. 109). It does not matter if larger pieces of plaster fall from the Kingspan as this can add to the overall effect. Small fissures can be scribed into the plaster once it has completely dried, using a sharp knife and the pointed end of a nail or screw.

When the carving process has been completed the outcrops can be glued on to the dry framework using PVA glue. If you want to add some drystone walling to the scene, horizontal pieces of card should be added to the framework at this point, to provide a fixing for the walling (Fig. 110). The pieces of card on which the walls will sit are glued in position at

Fig. 109. A toothbrush is used to remove any edges that are too sharp in appearance.

Fig. 110. Drystone walls are fixed in place.

Fig. 111. A small piece of ceiling tile is added to the screwed-up newspaper.

Fig. 112. Newspaper is pushed in among the outcrops.

almost the same level as the finished groundwork will be. This avoids hiding too much of the wall below ground level. These wall sections come on a pre-cast mound of earth, which will be blended in to the landscape as the scenic work progresses.

Tightly screwed-up newspaper is added inside the framework and it is this that will hold the hard shell of plaster-coated paper in place. Newspaper is very lightweight and easy to shape, which makes it an ideal but often overlooked material for forming hillsides.

A small length of ceiling tile is snapped rather than cut and then added to the groundwork (Fig. 111). Snapping this sort of ceiling tile gives very fine layers, which, when painted, look very much like the exposed earth that results from small landslides. Landslides like this are common on this sort of hillside, due partly to the crumbly nature of the rocks beneath the surface.

Rocky hillsides such as this often have a large, steep area of exposed rock that is sparsely covered with grass. This section is formed using the same methods as for the outcrops. When it has been coated with plaster and carved, it can be glued on to the baseboard and the gaps around it can be filled with more screwed-up newspaper (Fig. 112).

To lay the first layer of hard shell, paper strips soaked in diluted PVA glue (approximately 1 part glue to 1 part water) are placed over the screwed-up newspaper. Two or three layers are enough. Lay

the paper right up to the outcrops and try to avoid leaving any gaps. Next, mix more plaster – enough to give the whole surface of the hillside a thin coat – and apply with a large paintbrush. Use a knife or spatula to fill in any small gaps that may be present between the outcrops and the layers of paper.

Even at this stage (Fig. 113) the benefits of burying the base of the outcrops beneath the surface are evident, as they really do look like they are sticking up from beneath the groundwork.

Take the plastic sheet or bag that has had plaster spread on to it. Carefully fold part of the sheet or bag

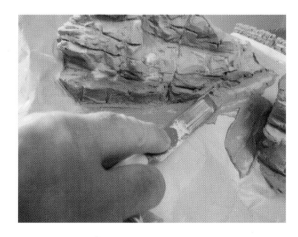

Fig. 113. Gaps are filled in with plaster.

Fig. 114. Once the plaster has dried, the outcrops can be painted.

Fig. 115. Small boulders and rocks are coloured to match the outcrops.

to loosen the plaster and break it up into various-sized pieces. Use PVA glue to stick some of the larger pieces on to the hillside. These pieces will look more natural if they are positioned below and around the outcrops, as if they are lying where they have fallen. Keep the rest of the sheet of plaster for later.

Leave the hillside to dry. When dry, the hard shell will be extremely tough and ready for the detailing steps.

PAINTING

Once the plaster has dried, the rocky outcrops and rock face can be painted. Thin washes of enamel paints are added and allowed to spread over the surface, which results in natural-looking rock formations. AK Interactive enamels have been used here. Thinned Dark Mud enamel has been brushed into the crevices to give shady areas to the sandstone (Fig. 114). The exposed faces and corners have been dry brushed with light earth pigments to add some tonal difference. Once these have dried, the whole rock face is given a wash of AK Interactive Slimy Grime Light and Slimy Grime Dark enamels, which gives a realistic weathered look to the sandstone.

The hillside will be covered with static grass so it is important to paint the surface of the hill to hide the colour of the plaster, otherwise it will show

through after the fibres have been added. A mid-brown matt emulsion paint, diluted 1 part paint to 1 part water, was used for the example; a suitable green paint would work equally well, and one coat should be enough. Take care when painting so as to not accidentally get any on your painted outcrops or rock faces. Leave the emulsion paint to dry.

Take the remainder of the plastic sheet with the plaster spread on it and gently screw it up, so that the plaster flakes away from the plastic into pieces of random thicknesses and sizes. Put the flakes into a container and add some of the paints that were used to paint the outcrops, carefully mixing well so that all surfaces of the flakes are covered (Fig. 115). Pour the flakes out on to another plastic sheet and set them aside to dry.

The exposed edge of the ceiling tile can now be painted, using AK Interactive Earth Effects enamel and a light coat of Dark Earth pigment. Brush some Treemendus Earth Powder on to the landslide and glue some to the area below the landslide too. The Earth Powder below the landslide has been put on thickly by mixing it with PVA and has been shaped by dragging a wooden skewer through it in one direction away from the tile, to give the impression that it has fallen away from the landslide (Fig. 116). Once the mixture has dried a little, roughen up its surface using a toothbrush or wooden skewer to add more texture.

Fig. 116. Adding texture to the landslide.

GRASS

The grass for this hillside is comprised mostly of Noch static grass fibres. Using just one length and colour of fibres results in an over-manicured effect, which is fine if you are modelling a well-tended lawn but not suitable for fields, meadows and natural hillsides. Using a variety of fibres gives a far more pleasing result.

A thick layer of static grass glue is applied using a paintbrush to the surface of the hillside. This glue is not ordinary PVA. Instead, its consistency keeps the pores on the surface of the glue open for longer,

Fig. 117. Glue in place ready for the static grass fibres.

which is ideal for catching and holding the charged fibres in a vertical position when they land and whilst they dry. Glue is also added to some of the flat surfaces of the rock face itself using a small paintbrush (Fig. 117). These areas will also be given a layer of static grass.

A small screw or hook is screwed into the hard plaster shell and the crocodile clip attached to the Noch Gras-Master applicator is fixed to the screw.

Before adding any grass fibres to the glue, take the flakes of painted plaster prepared earlier and sprinkle them on to the hillside. Most of this debris will be found below the outcrops from where it has fallen, but pieces of stone such as these can be seen anywhere on the surface of the hillside poking up through the grass. I find it best to simply drop them on to the glue and leave them where they come to rest; any pieces that look unnaturally placed can be removed.

The next step is to add the static grass fibres. Short summer green and wild grass fibres are blended together at a ratio of approximately 50/50 and are added to the hillside first, followed by various colours of short fibres. Next, longer fibres are added in a random fashion to produce small areas of longer grass. Finally, long fibres are applied around the outcrops, up against the drystone wall and in clumps

Fig. 118. A worn area around the gateway.

around the hillside. The entrance to the field behind the wall has been purposely kept clear of long fibres. This is because areas such as gateways tend to be worn more than the surrounding grass due to movement of livestock, people and farming vehicles. A sprinkle of Earth Powder and fine scatter will help to blend the worn gateway and the taller static grass together (Fig.118).

To finish off this step, use your fingertip to gently press into the glue all the small pieces of plaster that were sprinkled on to the hillside before the static grass was added. Allow the hillside to dry, then carefully remove all the loose static grass fibres using a vacuum cleaner.

A light dusting of Earth Powder can also be applied to other areas of the groundwork to give the hillside characteristic bare patches. Earth Powder sprinkled around the area below the landslide, to blend it into the static grass (Fig. 119), also adds to the impression that there has been recent movement to the ground.

Fig. 119. The landslide detail.

Fig. 120. Preparing Canopy material for the heathers.

ADDING VARIETY

Heather often grows in abundance on rocky hillsides such as the one being modelled here. The following method provides a simple way of creating heather, but also applies to all manner of low-growing foliage. Flowering plants of any kind can add a splash of colour to the landscape and are useful for drawing the eye to a particular feature on the layout, whether it be a garden, allotment, stretch of embankment or, in this case, a rocky outcrop. Making individual plants is not necessary as heather tends to grow in a 'carpet' on a hillside such as this.

To create the canopy for the foliage to sit on, you can use Treemendus Canopy material, a synthetic hair that comes in the form of a plait. Pinch a small amount of the fibres between your forefinger and thumb and pull them from the plait. Tease the fibres into an open structure – the more the material is teased and pulled, the more open the structure. Heathers are fairly dense-growing plants in the wild so it is a good idea to pull the Canopy apart and then roll it up into denser clumps. The clumps are then cut in half using scissors, placed flat side down, then pushed together to give a good representation of many plants growing tightly together side by side (Fig. 120). This process is repeated as many times as it takes until you have enough to cover the area that requires 'planting'.

The next step is to add the foliage to the heather. Spray the whole structure on both sides using hairspray; this will hold the leaves in place while the heather is being constructed. For the leaves, sprinkle on a blend of Treemendus fine Pine scatter and fine Mid Summer scatter. The Pine scatter is added first, followed by another misting of hairspray and then a light sprinkle of Mid Summer scatter. This gives an impression of new growth among the darker leaves (Fig. 121).

To add colour to the heather, spray the Canopy once more with hairspray, then apply a layer of suitably coloured scatter to represent flowers (Fig. 122). The flowers can be scattered either to give a light splash or a heavy mass of colour. Remember it is

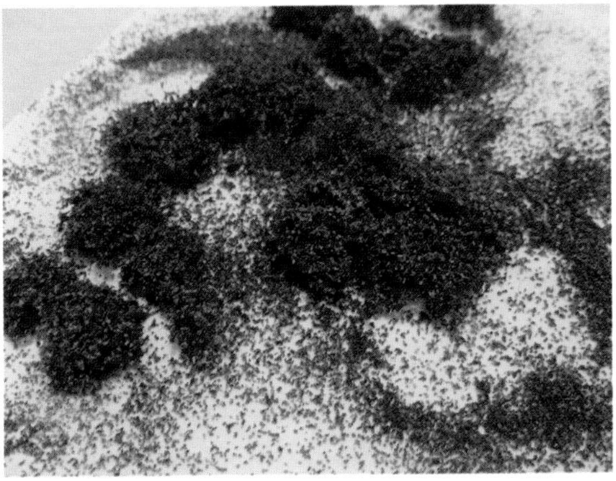

Fig. 121. Green scatter added to the Canopy.

Fig. 122. Flowers added to the heathers.

Fig. 123. The heather can now be added to the groundwork.

easier to add scatter than to remove it, so you may prefer to apply coloured scatter in stages rather than in one go. This way you can control how much colour will be visible on your layout.

The heather can now be positioned on to the landscape and should be carefully worked into the static grass (Fig. 123). A small spot of glue will help it stay in position. When it is sitting well among the grass, it can be given a spray of scenic glue. Not only will this hold the scatter securely, it will also fix the heather on to the groundwork.

Very finely chopped Raw Grass fibres may be added around the heather to help blend it in with the ground-work. The same fibres are also added around some of the stones that scatter the hillside (Fig. 124). Give everything a misting of hairspray to hold it in place.

Fig. 124. Raw Grass fibres are used to blend the heather and rocks into the static grass.

For a little more variety in the groundwork, individual nettles may be added. These kinds of weeds are very simple to make and are a very effective way of adding some extra height and colour among the grasses and rocks that cover the surface of the hill.

Cut a few bristles from a cheap nylon-bristled decorator's paintbrush. Black ones, ideally around 2in (5cm) in length are very suitable for the stems of nettles. Spread some neat PVA glue on to a sheet of paper and roll each bristle individually in the glue so as to cover it with a thin layer. Next, roll each bristle in a suitably coloured fine scatter – do not be too concerned about trying to cover the whole bristle with the scatter as in nature some nettles are more sparsely covered in leaves than others. Put the treated bristles to one side and allow them to dry with their tips resting on a piece of dowel. This will stop them from sticking to the paper while they dry (Fig. 125).

When the glue has dried and the scatter is held firmly in place, the nettles can be added to the groundwork. Begin by cutting each bristle approximately in half – allow for some variety in height, as this will add to the realism. Take one 'nettle' and hold it firmly with a pair of tweezers. Dip one end into neat PVA and work it into the static grass fibres (Fig. 126). Repeat this process to create small clumps of nettles. It may take some time to complete this step but it is well worth persevering with, as the effect really does add to the look of the scenery. Groups of nettles can be placed on the groundwork at the same time by holding a bunch of them with the tweezers and fixing them in the same way as the single stems.

If required, once they are securely stuck in place, the nettles can be trimmed using sharp scissors to reduce their height.

Fig. 125. Nettles are very easy to produce.

Fig. 126. Once dry, the nettles are added to the hillside.

THE DEAD TREE

Dead trees, or what is left of them, are another common feature of landscapes such as this. There are many good reference books on the subject of making and styling trees and a variety of methods can be adopted when it comes to making your own. Gordon Gravett's *Modelling Trees*, Part One (broadleaf) and Part Two (conifers) are particularly recommended. In particular, dead trees are simple to make and offer a good introduction to making trees in general – most of the fine branches will have fallen off, leaving only the weather-worn larger boughs remaining.

Before starting work on any tree it is very important to visualize how tall it will need to be to fit in with the other features in the surrounding area. Remember to make it slightly smaller if it is being placed towards the back of the layout, as this can add to the perspective of the scene. A tree of approximately 5in (12.5cm) in height will fit this scene perfectly; in 1:76 scale, that equates to around 30ft (9m). Only the remaining dead boughs are modelled and the tree would have been much taller when it was alive. Trees are often modelled well under scale but it is always advisable to make them to scale where possible.

This example uses the wire, bark powder and scenic glue included in a Treemendus tree kit. The wires in the kit are supplied in 12in (30cm) lengths.

Fig. 127. Trim wires into approximately 6in (15cm) lengths.

For a tree of this style and size, take around thirty or so wires and cut them in half (Fig. 127). There is no need to measure these cuts – somewhere in the centre of the wires will be fine. Gather the wires together and tap one end on a hard surface so that it becomes flat. Pull a few of the central wires out from the flat end of the main bunch and wrap a 2in (5cm) length of masking tape around them. These wires will become the planting pin, which will be used to fix the tree securely to the groundwork.

Next, tightly wrap a 4in (10cm) length of masking tape around the bottom of the 'trunk', to help hold the wires together securely and to make the process of building the wire armature easier. If you want to make a root system, position the 4in (10cm) length of masking tape approximately 1in (2.5cm) up the trunk and create the roots by twisting the wires in the same way as you would when forming the branches. Bend the lower trunk by hand to give more character to the tree.

Take a single strand of wire and coil it around what will become the trunk of the tree. Work the wire further up the trunk as you coil, until you get to the point where you want the first bough. Pull the wire tightly, as it is this wire that holds the trunk together initially.

Separate ten to fifteen wires and bend them downwards and outwards. These wires are your first bough. Continue winding the wire that was being coiled up your trunk around the bough. Now separate a few of the wires again; these will now become one of the side branches. Create branch systems by continually separating the wires and making side branches on alternate sides of the main boughs until all the wires have been used. In this instance, with this being a dead tree, these branch systems will actually be removed from the main tree and be placed in the grass at ground level to represent fallen boughs.

Take another wire and coil it around the trunk to add another bough to the opposite side of the tree. Repeat this process until all the wires have been used (Fig. 128).

Covering the wire with masking tape serves two purposes. First, it helps to hide the wires running

Fig. 128. A basic tree is constructed.

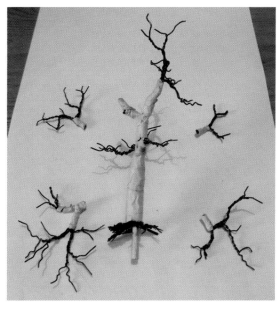

Fig. 129. Masking tape is applied to the tree and the branches are snipped off.

up the trunk and lower boughs, which can look unrealistic if they are visible once the tree is finished. Second, it is very useful for bulking up the trunk and lower boughs of the tree and helps you to create a tree with a larger-girthed trunk. Pull the masking tape tightly around the wire. Once this step has been completed, the shape and style of the dead tree are instantly recognizable.

If the look you want is a tree with only dead branches remaining attached to its trunk, chop off most of the side branches using wire cutters and leave a few finer branches in place (Fig. 129).

To simulate bark, with Treemendus Bark Powder, put a small amount of the powder into a container, add a small amount of scenic glue and mix the two together to form a thick paste. Apply this paste directly to the masking tape using a paintbrush (Fig. 130). Start applying the bark to the top of the tree first, as this allows you to hold the main trunk as you work. Leaving a large section of the masking tape around the trunk exposed will give the impression that the bark has been stripped away from this area and give the tree even more character. Leave the

Fig. 130. Coat the trunk and branches with Treemendus Bark Powder.

Fig. 131. Fine scatter has been fixed to the tree to represent moss.

coating of bark to dry. Once it has dried the tree will be very durable and ready to take a coat of paint.

Tree trunks, especially those of dead trees, are very rarely, if ever, brown. They usually range from grey to green in nature and often display a variety of colours, not a single one. The tree can be painted using watercolours or acrylic paints, which are best diluted to allow some of the bark detail to show through. In the example, a wash of ordinary watercolours was used for the bark and emulsion paint for the exposed heartwood. There are no hard and fast rules when it comes to mixing the paints – try putting a little water on to a saucer or a shallow container and add various shades of grey, green and a little brown. The paint is applied using a firm paintbrush, with the whole tree given a wash of watercolour. Whilst the wash is still wet, add some streaks and spots of undiluted paint and let it spread across the bark. Tiny amounts of dark paint can be dotted on to the trunk too.

The area of masking tape on the trunk and the tips of the branches are given a coat of emulsion paint. The mix for this is white emulsion, a drop of black poster paint and a couple of drops of yellow ochre poster paint. The yellow ochre adds a little warmth to the mix. Paint this on to the masking tape with a fine paintbrush and avoid getting it on the bark. Add some to the tips of the branches too. When the tree has dried, add some AK Interactive

Fig. 132. The tree is glued on to the hillside. Scenic glue is added around the root system.

Fig. 133. Scatter and Earth Powder help blend the roots into the hillside.

Slimy Green light acrylic to the heartwood and the bark of the tree.

Finally, paint neat PVA glue on to the upper sides of some of the branches and sprinkle it with a fine scatter to represent moss growing on the dead tree (Fig. 131). The addition of some scatter to the drystone wall next to the tree will create a visual interaction between the two.

Pierce a small hole into the plaster hard shell and push the tree's planting pin into it. The tree can be held in place using neat PVA, superglue or epoxy resin (Fig. 132). Scenic glue is added around the root system in anticipation of the following step. The boughs that were cut off the tree are coated with the bark mixture and painted using the same method as the tree, and added to the groundwork. A little spot of glue holds them in place.

In order to blend the tree's root system into the existing groundwork, use some of the finely chopped

> **Tip**
>
> For trees that need to be removed from the layout from time to time, for example, for storage or when taking the layout to exhibitions, glue a 3mm-diameter brass or aluminium tube to the tree's planting pin. Then insert and glue a 4mm-diameter tube into the baseboard. Slide the tree into the tube on the baseboard and it will stay securely in place until it needs to be lifted out.

Raw Grass fibres and Earth Powder. Take some of the fibres and soak them with scenic glue. Use a wooden skewer to work them into and around the tree's roots (Fig. 133). A light sprinkling of Earth Powder and a few long static grass fibres complete the 'planting' process.

Fig. 134. The completed scene: 55 022 heads south with an Edinburgh to King's Cross train.

THE COMPLETED DIORAMA

Hillsides with these characteristics are fairly common and lend themselves well to layouts based on many regions of the UK. A tall rocky outcrop is a useful way of disguising the point where a train leaves the fiddle yard to enter a scenic part of your layout (Fig. 134). An animal appears to have made its home in the loose earth around the landslide, a huge rotten branch lies downhill from the tree from which it fell, and the telegraph pole that runs alongside the railway indicates that the scene is not far away from civilization. It is the little features like this that bring the scene to life.

SUMMARY

Lightweight corrugated cardboard, newspaper, Kingspan and finishing plaster are the four main materials that were used to construct the hard shell in this example. By using various colours of static grass in differing lengths, great grass effects can be achieved. By mixing other materials among the grass fibres, the effects can be enhanced even further. The scene is one of grass and stone but there are many more tiny features that do not at first jump out at the viewer. That is what can make scenes like this more interesting than they might first appear.

Fig. 135. Class A1 60114 W.P. Allen steams through the countryside. Note how the colours of the rocks and grasses blend together to bring visual harmony either side of the track.

CHAPTER FIVE

STEEP CLIFF FACES

Fig. 136. A cliff face in west Wales.

Materials

- Ply board (3mm)
- Ceiling tiles
- Polystyrene
- PVA glue/grab adhesive
- Cement
- Plaster
- Emulsion paint
- Scenic modelling materials
- Paints/weathering powders

Tools

- Steel rule
- Scalpel/Stanley knife
- Sandpaper
- Large paintbrush
- Assorted small paintbrushes

There are a number of techniques that can be used to model realistic cliff faces. The cliff face here contains two very different-looking types of rock – one layer set vertically and one horizontally – which adds interest in respect of texture and colouring. The caves add further interest to the cliff face. The geology beneath the earth is an amazing record of how the landscape has formed over millions of years. When tectonic plates collide, albeit very slowly, they have a profound effect on what happens at the surface. Steep cliff faces, which at a glance appear to be just one kind of rock, can be made up from many completely different types that have been forced together. These layers of rock can be bent and twisted and set at all sorts of angles. Modelling cliff faces based on this kind of geological activity can be fascinating.

In areas with steep cliff faces, rock falls can be common. These can involve an individual rock or a group of rocks falling down the slope, and large

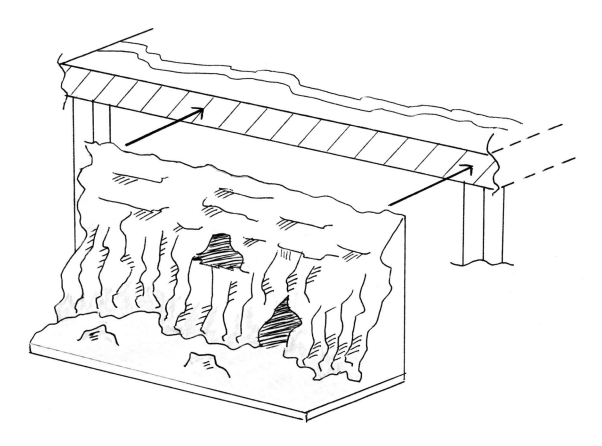

Fig. 137. Line drawing showing how cliff faces can be used at the front of the layout, below baseboard level.

rocks in turn may dislodge other rocks. Over time the debris that gathers at the bottom of the slope may vary enormously in size, from large boulders to tiny fragments. This is a feature that can be added to a model in order to capture the environment that you are aiming to re-create.

The simple rock face in the example combines all the elements mentioned above. Plants and weeds always find pockets in which to grow and even trees can grow from surprisingly small cracks in the solid rock.

PREPARATION

The example features a steep cliff that towers over a beach. If you are building a steep cliff and intend to run a railway at the bottom of it, remember to measure

and allow clearance for your stock (see Chapter 1). A cliff face built using the following method will be very lightweight and look great at the front of a layout, hanging down below the baseboard level. This gives the impression that everything modelled at baseboard level is in fact on top of a steep cliff. It would only need to be proud from the front of the layout by a few inches too, so it should not take up much valuable space. Alternatively, it could be added at a later date, without interfering with the rest of the layout. A coastal path leading from a country lane could run along the front edge of the baseboard. A single- or double-track railway on an embankment could follow the path of the lane. To the rear of the layout the cliff face could be repeated and this would act as a dramatic backdrop to the whole scene.

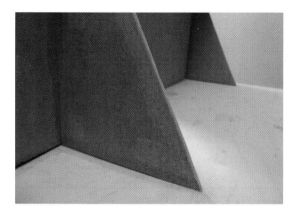

Fig. 138. Ply wedges hold the cliff face vertical. A more substantial frame may be required in some cases.

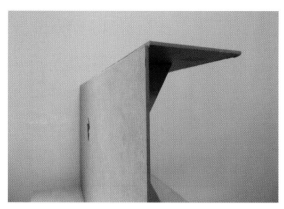

Fig. 139. The horizontal ply represents the baseboard level.

If you choose to use this method of constructing a cliff face at the front of your baseboard, it is recommended that you screw ply to the front of the layout and work directly on to it, in situ. In the example, the ply is attached to a simple frame, of the type that can be built anywhere on the layout.

The basic framework for this diorama was made using 3mm ply board. The vertical surface has been set at ninety degrees, as this is the angle it would probably be at if attached to the front of most layouts. The ply wedges holding it in place can of course be cut at any angle (Fig. 138). The horizontal ply at the top represents the front of the baseboard at layout level (Fig. 139). Fix a piece of board to the bottom of the vertical face to give the cliff something to sit on. This piece sticks out only 6in (15cm) and will be modelled in the style of a beach but you could have another track running there instead.

Two holes have been cut out of the vertical piece of ply board, one at ground level and another about halfway up the cliff (Fig. 140). These holes will be turned into caves in the cliff face, thereby adding another feature to the scenery.

Fig. 140. Holes are made in the board. These will become cave entrances.

Fig. 141. The wire armature is added to the cliff, but not glued in at this point.

Fig. 142. Snapped compressed paper ceiling tiles are the material used for the lower layer of rock.

Trees can take root in small fissures on cliff faces and to achieve this effect a wire armature is fixed directly through a small hole in the ply (Fig. 141). It will be coated in bark and given its canopy of foliage once the main construction process is complete. Do not glue it in place at this stage, as it will be necessary to remove it while constructing the upper layers of rock.

CREATING ROCK LAYERS AND CAVES

The layers of rock for the cliff are created from pieces of compressed paper ceiling tile, snapped by hand into short lengths and random sizes. Pieces from a sheet of polystyrene are also used, to represent different layers of rock among the ceiling tiles (Fig. 142). The lower layer of rock on the cliff is placed almost vertically above this – the layers are to be positioned roughly horizontally. Ceiling tiles are used to represent the upper layer of rock and pieces of polystyrene can also be used for this kind of work.

This cliff face differs from a man-made cutting in appearance, because of the nature of the rock formation. There will naturally be areas of rock protruding from the cliff and these are modelled using ceiling tiles. Take three or four pieces of tile, trim them flat at their base and their back and glue them directly to the ply board at whatever angle you like. In the example, they have been glued at an angle of around eighty degrees (Fig. 143). These form the cliff face at the furthest point you want it to protrude from the vertical ply. They do not have to be all the same depth; a certain randomness will add to the realism of the cliff.

Use neat PVA glue or grab adhesive to hold the first pieces in place. Do not position them equal distances apart as this may look unrealistic when the whole cliff is complete (Fig. 144). Do try to space them so that the gaps may be filled according to the width of the ceiling tile. Note that the bottom of each piece is trimmed at the desired angle; here, the pieces are trimmed so that they sit at eighty degrees.

Fig. 143. One of the main pieces of wall set at approximately an eighty-degree angle.

Fig. 144. Allow these pieces to dry before adding the remaining pieces.

Fig. 145. The tiles are positioned to produce little coves and outcrops along its base.

It is important to allow these pieces of ceiling tile to dry before moving on to the next step, which involves filling in the spaces between the near vertical pieces of tile that are already fixed to the ply. Ideally, you need to find pieces of tile that are similar in shape to the one to which you are gluing. These additional pieces of tile do not have to be glued to the vertical piece of ply at any point, as long as they are fixed securely to the adjacent piece.

Fig. 146. A natural-looking cave entrance in the cliff face.

Work your way along the outer edge of each of the main pieces of tile that were fixed in place earlier, forming little rocky features as you work. Each of the additional pieces that are added should be positioned a little further back from the previously added piece, so as to take the cliff face back towards the ply board and thus create small coves (Fig. 145).

Caves need not be particularly deep – some are just a few feet in depth. To create a natural-looking cave entrance, the cliff face is constructed by working the ceiling tile pieces back towards the hole in the ply board. Pieces of tile are now glued vertically behind the ply alternately from left and right. Gradually, a cave is formed as the tiles meet (Fig. 146). Glue some pieces of tile to fill the gap at the top of the cave, forming a roof. Note how the cave appears to be a natural hollow in the cliff as opposed to a hole in the ply board.

To add an almost horizontal seam of rock on top of the vertical layer (Fig. 147), use polystyrene, to give some textural difference between the two types of rock. Add a layer of ceiling tiles on top of the polystyrene, this time placed horizontally. These horizontal pieces of ceiling tile must be glued to the ply board. Another cave – this time a very shallow hollow in the cliff face – may be created using the same method (Fig. 148).

Fig. 147. To give the cliff more character, the upper layer of rock is laid horizontally above the vertical layer.

Allow the PVA holding the horizontal layer of tiles to dry. The tiles can then be shaped and sanded to create a rock face that is smoother-looking than the vertical layer below it. Blades, sandpaper, fingers and a toothbrush can be used when carving this type of tile. Have a vacuum cleaner to hand as this is a messy process. It is also advisable to wear a dust mask as you proceed with this step.

Filling in the gaps between the tiles will help the appearance of the cliff. Small pieces of tile can be pushed into the gaps by hand. This layer is given a very thin coat of the cement mixture described in Chapter 2 (1 part PVA to 2 parts water, plus enough cement to create a thin paste). Apply the mixture to the upper level of the cliff face and the polystyrene layer using a wide paintbrush. If you want to smooth

Fig. 148. A small cave is added to the upper wall. Little features like this can add greatly to the end result.

Fig. 149. Carving the tiles helps with the overall look of the cliff face.

the surface, run a wet paintbrush horizontally over the surface as it dries. The cement should be allowed to dry before the painting process begins.

Meanwhile, use a sharp blade to take away any unnatural-looking bits of tile that may be sticking out too far from the vertical layer of rock in the cliff face (Fig. 149). If necessary, add some detail around the mouths of the caves, again by carving away the tile. Next, seal the whole cliff face, using diluted PVA (5 parts water to 1 part PVA), and allow it to dry completely before the next step. Sealing the surface of the tiles will prevent them from flaking and breaking away over time.

PAINTING

Once the cement mixture and the diluted PVA primer have dried, the whole structure can be given an undercoat. Here, the undercoat used was black poster paint with a tiny bit of white poster paint added and diluted by approximately 1 part paint to 6 parts water. Black never really occurs in nature and the overall result is better when the black is lightened, even if it is just a tiny bit. Diluted acrylic paints can be used for painting the cliff instead, if you prefer. Most of this undercoat will be painted over with progressively lighter tones of paint but the

deepest fissures and inside the caves are purposely left very dark (Fig. 150).

The aim of this application of paint is to shade all the cracks, fissures and the inside of the caves, so do not be alarmed if the cliff face appears too dark at this early stage. As the paint dries the whole surface of the cliff will lighten. It is then dry brushed with varied tones of paint, to pick out all the surface detail in the cement mixture and the ceiling tiles and add to the effect of the steep cliff face.

To add detail to the rock face it is best to give it a few coats of paint that get lighter in tone as each layer is added. There is no real science behind the way paint is applied to these types of cliff. If you study photographs of the real thing, you will see there can be all sorts of colours and patterns occurring naturally on steep cliff faces, so a random application of paints can give equally good results when compared to strategic painting.

When the undercoat is dry, lighter tones of paint can be painted on to the surface of the cliff face. The lighter tones are applied using the dry-brushing method, as used on the cutting wall in Chapter 2. When dry brushing, paint is applied to the tip of the brush then most of it is wiped off on to a tissue or piece of cloth. The paint is then applied to the cliff face. As there is only a small amount of paint

Fig. 150. The whole cliff is initially painted using a very dark undercoat, which must be left to dry. Progressively lighter shades of paint are then dry brushed over the undercoat.

Fig. 151. Introducing brown and green patches to the upper cliff face adds to the overall effect.

on the bristles, the dark undercoated fissures in the tiles retain their shadowy colour. Apply the paint in horizontal strokes to the vertical tiles at the foot of the cliff; as with the painting of the rock on other projects, this ensures that the tiny fissures in the tiles retain their dark shady undercoat. Vertical strokes can be used on the upper layer of rock to add further visual difference to the two layers.

The three paint mixes for dry brushing are very similar to those described in Chapter 2, but have slightly more black content. The main paint for the mixes is matt white emulsion and it is advisable to mix three different shades based on the same paint colours:

- Mix 1: 8 parts matt white; 3 parts yellow; 3 parts black.
- Mix 2: 8 parts matt white; 2 parts yellow; 2 parts black.
- Mix 3: 10 parts matt white; 1 part yellow; 1 part black.

The three tones should be mixed to suit the type of rock being modelled. Sandstone, for example, will have a more orange colour to it. As the paints are applied it will become apparent that mixing three or more different shades of a similar colour will give

realistic variety to the cliff. The different tones of paint will add to the light and shade effect on the cliff, whilst ensuring that the colours blend together well.

This process is best done in stages, allowing each layer of paint to dry before applying the next lighter tone. Dry brush the whole wall with horizontal strokes using the darker shade of paint then start again using a lighter shade. As you work along the cliff, you can dry brush small amounts of green and brown emulsion paint to the upper layers of rock (Fig. 151).

Fig. 152. Using horizontal brush strokes across the grain of the tile ensures the dark undercoat remains visible in the fissures throughout the cliff face.

Fig. 153. More shade can be added to the bottom of the overhanging ledges by dry brushing dark tones of paint to the underside of the ledges.

When applying the lightest shade of paint to the lower level of rock, use horizontal strokes (Fig. 152). This action prevents the tiny fissures from being filled with lighter-coloured paint and helps the cliff to retain its realistic texture. It also adds to the impression of rock on the cliff that has been exposed to the harsh elements associated with coastal regions. Note how a horizontal fault line has been carved out of the tiles to add extra detail to the lower cliff face.

Shading the underside of any overhangs on the cliff face using a dark paint is an effective way of introducing shadows to the cliff (Fig. 153).

This cliff rises vertically from a beach, so, to add to the impression of the effects of the tide, a high-tide mark is painted at its base. Areas of rock that are continually in and out of seawater often discolour and have seaweed and barnacles growing on them. Such water marks are not only caused by seawater – any features along the edge of lakes, rivers, streams and canals, where the water level can rise and fall even slightly, can also display this type of weathering.

Apply a band of paint approximately 1in (2.5cm) high along the base of the cliff (Fig. 154). This band is darker than the rest of the cliff face and gives the impression that it is still wet. Weathering pigments and enamel paints can be used to add to the effect

Fig. 154. A feature of coastal cliffs is a high-tide mark, represented by a band of paint at the very base of the cliff.

Tip

It is always advisable to paint a test piece first and then allow it to dry to see if you have achieved the colour of rock that you want. Further coats of paint can then be added until the desired effect has been captured.

Fig. 155. Weathering materials – here, Slimy Green – are added to the high-tide mark. They are best added in vertical brush strokes.

of the high-tide mark (Fig. 155). These areas look better if the paint and pigments are all applied with vertical brush strokes.

The seaweed that sometimes grows on a cliff face at sea level can be of the brightest green. One way of replicating this is to apply neat PVA glue to the top of the high-tide line on the cliff face and sprinkle Fine Spring Green scatter on to the glue (Fig. 156). When the glue has dried, the loose scatter can be either brushed away or removed with a vacuum cleaner.

Although the cliff face has been painted to represent weathered rock, it will benefit from some more weathering, and AK Interactive pigments and enamels are perfect for this type of work. Although they are designed with the weathering of vehicles in mind, they are more than suitable for use on scenery. Fresh Mud, Earth Effects, Slimy Grime Light and Dark Enamels, European Earth and Dark Earth pigments can all be used to subtly weather the cliff.

Fig. 156. Seaweed often grows along high-tide marks. Bright green scatter can represent the kind of weed found in such places.

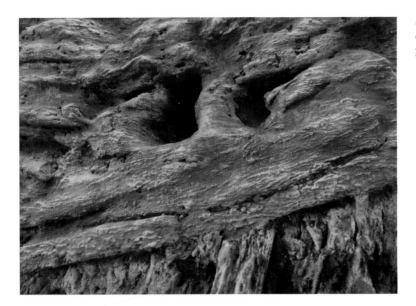

Fig. 157. Weathering powders are used to create more features on the cliff face.

The weathering pigments are applied using small paintbrushes. Vertical strokes work well as they give the impression of the action of rainwater and other elements, which over time leave streaks on the rock (Fig. 157).

Sometimes a cliff such as this may be covered in lichen and can display the most vivid of golden colours. One way of adding lichen is by applying oil paint with a short-bristled brush. The effect will be better if the paint is dabbed on rather than being applied using brush strokes. Lightly cover the tips of the bristles with the paint and work your way randomly across the cliff face. Paint some of the paint along the top of the tidal mark to highlight the difference in the two features (Fig. 158). In the example, Lemon Yellow with tiny dabs of Crimson were blended together for the lichen effect.

Fig. 158. Lemon Yellow oil paint can be used to great effect when it comes to covering the cliff with a realistic coating of lichen. Tiny dabs of Crimson oil paint are randomly added to the yellow as the painting process is undertaken.

Fig. 159. Fine scatters, static grass fibres and Earth Powder all add to the effect of a rugged cliff face. Hairspray and scenic glue hold them in place.

The next step concentrates on the upper layer of rock in the cliff. Although the rock in the upper layer has been painted to look similar in colour to the layer below it, it will benefit from having some moss and grass added to the cracks and crevices. Fix Treemendus fine Spring and Mid Summer scatters to the wall using Scenefix glue or diluted PVA glue (3 parts water to 1 part glue). Static grass fibres may also be added to some of the ledges that are in between the layers of rock. Sprinkle them on to the glue by hand, and then sprinkle a little Earth Powder on to the glue holding the fibres in place. A liberal misting of hairspray will help to hold the scatters, fibres and powder in place (Fig. 159).

Treemendus Limestone Scree is added to the beach at the bottom of the cliff. It is similar in colour

Fig. 160. Treemendus Limestone Scree is added around the base of the cliff. When the glue dries it will be dry brushed with the paints used on the cliff face to match the colour of the cliff more closely.

Fig. 161. The tree can now be fixed in place on the cliff, pushed into the hole whilst the bark is still wet. This makes for a more realistic representation of a tree growing from a small crevice as opposed to being simply stuck in a hole.

to the rock on the cliff face and looks as though it has fallen naturally and been washed into place by the tide (Fig. 160). When the glue has dried, give the scree a light dry brushing using the same paints that were mixed to colour the cliff face. This will add to the impression that the rocks have fallen from above. A light covering of Treemendus fine Spring scatter helps blend it in to the high-tide mark.

The tree growing from the cliff is given a coat of Treemendus Bark Powder and can be glued in place (Fig. 161). Once the bark has dried to form a hard coating to the wire, a simple canopy of foliage can be created using the materials included in the tree kit. Tease the Canopy material apart using your fingers to form little mounds that are open and airy in structure. Spray them with ordinary hairspray, to hold the

Fig. 162. Once the bark has dried the tree canopy can be attached to the wire armature. A couple of spots of PVA help hold it in place.

Fig. 163. Sand is carefully added to the beach to finish the scene, but cliffs like this do not have to be rising from a beach. You can model the groundwork around the base to suit whatever location you want to replicate.

scatter in place whilst the tree's canopy of leaves is being made. Whilst the hairspray is still wet, lightly sprinkle on a scatter – choose a colour to suit the season being modelled.

Once you have made enough foliage canopies to cover the tree you have built, spray them with the glue included in the tree kit. This glue will help hold the scatter in the long term. Allow the foliage canopies to dry and tease the material apart again if necessary. They can then be attached to the wire armature using a couple of spots of PVA (Fig. 162).

The green of the foliage will contrast well with the golden colour of the lichen, adding even more interest to the landscape. Once the foliage is in position, you can give the whole tree a blast of hairspray,

which reacts with the glue and makes for a very sturdy tree.

The last element to model is the foot of the cliff. This can be modelled however you like – it could be a sandy beach, a pebbly beach, a rocky ravine or woodland, or it could have a track at its base, used for storage or display purposes or to allow for a simple continuous track running below the level of the main layout.

For a sandy beach, it might be useful to paint the board a suitable colour before applying the sand, for example, using the same cement mixture as was used to cover the cliff face. Any of the mixture that shows through the sand will look like rock just beneath the surface. Apply scenic glue thickly to the board, then sprinkle a blend of sand and tiny pieces of dark gravel

Fig. 164. All caves at sea level have some kind of rubbish or other in them. Wood often finds its way into caves around the coastline.

on to it (Fig. 163). Allow the glue to soak through the sand and try to avoid touching it as it sets. Carefully spray the whole surface with hairspray to help it soak up the glue. When this has dried it will be very durable.

Coastal caves at beach level always gather a varied mixture of driftwood, general rubbish and flotsam and jetsam. The back of the cave in the example was filled with tiny bits of strip wood, roots and small trimmings of natural branches to represent old tree trunks (Fig. 164).

THE COMPLETED DIORAMA

It is a hot summer's day at the beach in the example (Fig. 165). Realistic steep cliffs have been created and the lichen-covered lower layer of the cliff and the high-tide mark really add to the coastal feel of the scene. The tide is out, so it is possible to see that the rocks on the beach are of the same type as those on the cliff face. They look quite natural lying on the beach at the foot of the cliff.

Fig. 165. Bliss.

SUMMARY

This project is a representation of a small section of steep cliff face, the sort of rock formations that are found along the coast of Britain, as well as inland. Remember to study the actual rock formations in the area you have chosen to model, especially when it comes to getting the colours right. Most of the paints used here are either emulsion or poster paints; emulsion paints alone can be used to create these effects if mixed to the three tones. You may find a selection of sample-sized 'match pots' very useful when the time comes for you to create your cliff face.

Compressed paper ceiling tiles are a superb material when used in the construction of steep cliff faces. There are two distinct, very different layers of rock, both made using the ceiling tile; the upper layer is laid horizontally and coated in a cement slurry, which dries to a very durable rock face, while the lower layer is made simply by gluing snapped pieces of tile together to form a realistic-looking stretch of vertical standing rock.

Fig. 166. BR Ivatt Class 2MT 46400 hauls a coal train out of a tunnel into a shaft of sunlight. Steep cliffs can be incorporated into even the narrowest of layouts.

CHAPTER SIX

SNOWY MOUNTAIN TOPS

Fig. 167. Of course snow is white but its appearance can vary dramatically, depending on what lies underneath it, for example, mud, and the effect that light has on it.

Materials

- Polystyrene sheet
- Cement
- Cork granules
- PVA glue
- Dark poster/emulsion paint
- Scenic modelling materials
- Paints/weathering powders

Tools

- Steel rule
- Scalpel/Stanley knife
- Large paintbrush
- Small paintbrushes
- Wooden skewer

Mountain tops vary from region to region – some are very barren whilst others can be covered in lush grass or a blend of rocks and grass. Tall mountains retain a covering of snow throughout the year and a number of techniques may be used to model realistic snow-covered mountains.

A mountain is a raised part of the Earth's surface, formed over millions of years due to the movement of the Earth's crust and what lies beneath it. Many mountain ranges are still growing even today as movement below the surface pushes up new layers of rock. It is partly due to these movements that fragments of rock loosen and fall from the surface of the rock face, creating piles of scree at their feet. Mountains are much larger than hills and are often rockier in nature than rolling hillsides.

The elements are constantly changing the very fabric of the landscape. Water can shape the rock, often creating deep cuts in the mountainside where it runs day after day, year after year. If trees do manage to take a hold in these harsh conditions they can very often be blown into fascinating shapes, with all the branches growing away from the wind in the same direction, or windswept as they are known. Even the rocks themselves can gradually be shaped and weathered by the effects of the wind and rain. Often, even in the summer months, a thin layer of snow will remain in these mountainous areas. The techniques involved in replicating such landscapes will be of special interest to modellers making Alpine-based layouts.

PREPARATION

Any of the materials and building methods used in Chapters 3, 4 and 5 can be employed to create mountain tops, with a chicken-wire, card and newspaper or ply-board framework acting as the base. Sometimes the main reason that a mountain is added to a layout is in order to incorporate a mountain railway line. Mountain railways can run through seemingly impossible terrain and can be extremely picturesque. Layouts with this theme sometimes require the construction of a high-level track on a stable raised platform of board, which weaves

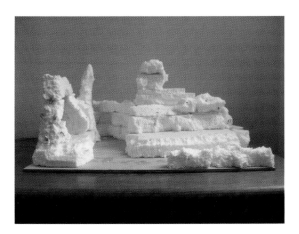

Fig. 168. The polystyrene sheets used in the construction of the terrain are both lightweight and easy to shape. Use the available space wisely, to create depth and interest to the scene.

through the rocky outcrops associated with the mountain. The example focuses on the actual building of the mountain peaks down to the ravine, which runs at the base of the mountain, albeit in a very condensed space.

The shape and size of the mountains you build will be determined by the space you have available on the layout. If height is not an issue in your railway room, then the mountain sides and peaks can be made to any scale, with tracks running at multiple levels. The taller the mountains are, the more it can add to their dramatic effect. Tunnel mouths or stacks of rock built in front of the track can help disguise exit points from the layout, where the trains leave the scenic part of the layout and join tracks out of sight of the viewer.

CONSTRUCTION

Polystyrene sheets are used to construct the basic terrain. The sheets are snapped into small pieces and arranged on top of each other to give a mountainous structure. It is advisable to take your time with the positioning of the polystyrene and to test the pieces in various positions. Stacks, caves, ravines and other rocky features can be sculpted by placing the pieces at different angles, so it is worth having a play around with their position before fixing them. Remember to account for the correct clearance for your trains between the track and the mountainside.

The pieces of polystyrene are glued together using PVA glue or grab adhesive and it is best to pin them together with small lengths of wire whilst the glue dries (Fig. 168).

Here, a small recess is cut out from the polystyrene either side of the ravine, for the foundations of a bridge to sit in.

When the glue holding the polystyrene together has dried, the small pieces of wire can be removed and the whole terrain structure can be given a coat of a cement mixture.

The mixture can be given extra texture with the addition of coarse cork granules. This is not obligatory but it provides a simple way of introducing

Preparing the coating

To create a realistic and durable surface for a rugged mountainside, you need to coat the structure with a blend of a few readily available materials. All measurements are approximate and should be mixed to a consistency to suit your terrain. The quantity below will be enough for an area approximately 24 x 24in (60 x 60cm).

In a container mix together 100ml of PVA glue and 500ml of clean cold water. To the liquid add three mugs of ordinary household cement and two mugs of cork granules (optional). Blend the liquid, cement and cork together until a thick creamy-textured paste has formed. Add more water or cement as required. The PVA will keep the mixture workable for quite a while but if you need to keep it workable for longer add a drop of washing-up liquid to the mix.

Fig. 169. Cork granules are added to the cement-based slurry to give the mountainside extra texture, and the mixture is then applied using a large paintbrush.

more texture to the surface of the rock. As you paint the mixture on to the polystyrene, using a large paintbrush (Fig. 169), you can see the marked textural effect that the cork granules will have on the surface of the mountainside.

The stack of rock to the left-hand side of the diorama makes for an interesting feature in its own right but is also a very useful shield, which allows trains to run from the scenic part of the layout into a position 'off stage' behind the scenes and into a fiddle yard (Fig. 170). As the stack is coated with the textured cement mixture, it starts to look more like a natural feature of the landscape.

Fig. 170. The textured coating can be used to fill in small gaps between the pieces of polystyrene, helping to create a more realistic rock structure.

Fig. 171. The base of the ravine can then be cleared of cork granules to give a smooth surface on which to add a stream.

The track will run across a small bridge, which spans a narrow gap over a deep mountain stream. (The cutaway section on either side of the ravine will house the bridge.) The floor and walls of the ravine are also given a coat of the textured cement mixture. Any gaps present between the polystyrene and the baseboard should be filled in with the mixture.

The course of a mountain stream has been cleared from the ravine (Fig. 171). Note how the stream enters the scene from the left and out of sight of the viewer, which suggests it actually comes from somewhere around the corner as opposed to simply running from the front of the layout to the back. This effect has been achieved by building a polystyrene wall to the rear of the stream and bending it round the back of the rock in front of the stream.

A wide, damp paintbrush is all that is required to remove the cork granules from the area where you want your stream to run. They could be left in place and poke through the surface of the water but in this instance I want a smooth bed for the water to run in. Of course the area where my stream flows could be modelled to resemble a dry stream bed where no water is running, a road or path, or a mixture of boulders and plants instead.

The cement should be left to dry before painting commences.

BUILDING THE BRIDGE

A small wooden bridge to span the gap over the ravine is an easy feature to build and a perfect way of taking trains across the gap. It can be built and painted away from the layout or in situ, as here.

Measure four lengths of 5mm square timber to fit across the gap. Glue two of the pieces into place, sufficiently far apart so that it will be wider than the track that will be laid over it. These two lengths of timber must be glued lower than the level of the polystyrene (track level), to allow for a piece of ply or, as in this case, thick card, to be fixed to the top of them. The top of the card must run flush with the

Fig. 172. A simple wooden bridge will take the track over the ravine. The first two pieces of timber are positioned below track level.

Fig. 173. Ply or card (as in this case) is glued to the top of the timbers. This is the base for the track to sit on and must be level with the terrain on either side of the gap.

Fig. 174. Two side pieces of timber are added, not only to strengthen the bridge, but also to stop the ballast from falling off the sides.

polystyrene, which will enable it to carry the track smoothly over the gap (Fig. 172).

Carefully measure a piece of thick card to the correct length of the gap, then measure and trim it widthwise so that it is 5mm narrower than the outside width of the two lengths of timber. Apply glue to the underside edges of the card and position it carefully on top of the timbers. Centre it on the timbers, leaving a 2.5mm gap on the outer edge of each (Fig. 173).

Add the two remaining lengths of timber to the bridge. Apply glue to the outer edges of the card and the top of the timber already in place. These timbers can be simply placed directly on the glue and will sit snugly in the recess created by the card and lower pieces of timber (Fig. 174).

Fig. 175. Plastic fencing is fixed in position on either side of the bridge.

Fig. 176. Diluted emulsion paints are washed over the surface of the rock, highlighting the texture created by adding cork to the coating.

Measure two pieces of plastic fencing to the correct length – the same length as the timber bridge (Fig. 175) – and fix one to either side of the bridge structure Drill small holes into the top of the timber so that the pins on the fence posts have something to sit in. A tiny drop of superglue holds them firmly in place. The bridge will be painted and weathered at a later stage.

ADDING COLOUR

Dry brushing (see Chapter 2) is a method of painting that would be well suited to achieving the texture of the rock in the example. Another way to achieve convincing effects is to use diluted emulsion paint, enamel paints and weathering pigments. Your choice of paint colour may be determined by the location on which your model is based, but generally you could go for three different mixes, as before:

- Mix 1: light-coloured emulsion, diluted 5 parts water to 1 part paint.
- Mix 2: dark-coloured emulsion, diluted 3 parts water to 1 part paint.
- Mix 3: 10 parts matt white, 1 part yellow and 1 part black, undiluted.

This method of painting is faster and somewhat easier than dry brushing as the paint is applied to the surface using a large paintbrush and allowed to find its own way down the rock structures. Note how much the emulsion paint has been diluted (Fig. 176). Apply the paint in random spots and streaks all over the mountain until the whole surface has received a thin coat. On the example, the lighter-coloured paint (Mix 1) was applied first, then dabbed off with a piece of tissue where necessary. This first coat does not need to cover the cement totally; the colour of the cement showing through the paints will add to the character of the mountain.

Next, dab on some of the darker paint (Mix 2) in areas underneath overhangs and around the walls of the ravine. When this has dried, check the result. It may be necessary to repeat the process in certain areas to get the look and strength of colour you require. Remember it is easier to add more paint than to take it off, so dilute it to a strength you are happy working with. Finally add some of the lighter paint (Mix 3) to the mountain. Mix 3 is best applied using the dry-brushing method.

At this stage the mountain will look a little bland in appearance but you should not be too concerned as there are more layers of texture and colour to be added.

Fig. 177. Gravel on the flat surfaces on the mountainside and around the course of the stream in the ravine adds even more texture to the landscape. It also helps to define the edges of the stream.

Fig. 178. Enamel paints are used to undercoat the bridge. An undercoat on the whole structure brings the different elements of the bridge together.

Fig. 179. Weathering helps to tone down the newness of the undercoat. Of course you are free to paint features like this any way you choose.

Mountains and rocky hillsides usually produce scree, which is a mixture of small stones, rocks and boulders that fall from the rock face from time to time and accumulate at their foot or on ledges. To replicate this, position gravel carefully in the relevant places on the landscape and work it into convincing lines along the edges of the ravine. The gravel is then sprayed with a liberal amount of hairspray and soaked with Scenefix glue, which will firmly hold it all in place once it has dried (Fig. 177).

While you are waiting for the glue holding the scree in place to dry, use the time to paint the bridge. To give the bridge more visual stability, you can add two load-bearing legs, made using the same timber as the horizontal timbers in the structure. Give the bridge structure a coat of paint that will serve as an undercoat, and leave it to dry. On the example, the bridge was painted using enamel paints in a colour that resembles bare wood (Fig. 178).

This is also a good point at which to ballast the track and fix it in place, first by spraying with hairspray and then by dribbling Scenefix glue on to the hairspray-soaked ballast.

To give the bridge a more realistic appearance, the next step involves weathering (Fig. 179). First, AK Interactive pigments and enamel paints are used to tone down the colour of the undercoat. As with many weathering techniques, vertical brush strokes work best, giving the impression of streaks where water runs down the bridge and into the stream below. Note the rust streaks on the side of the bridge.

IMPROVING THE LANDSCAPE

At this point the landscape still looks very barren as it is void of anything living. It can be greatly improved with the addition of just four simple groundwork materials: Earth Powder, two scatters and static grass fibres. To liven it up, Treemendus Earth Powder is added to all the flat surfaces on the mountainside, including the area running alongside the ballast (Fig. 180). Scenefix glue is brushed on to the areas where the Earth Powder is to be added, then the Earth Powder is sprinkled on to the glue and given a spray with hairspray.

To add some much-needed colour to the scene, scatter is added on top of the Earth Powder. Scenefix glue is dribbled over the Earth Powder and then Treemendus Late Summer fine scatter is sprinkled on to the glue (Fig. 181). Some more drops of glue are added on top of the Late Summer scatter, to enable a second colour of scatter – here, Treemendus Mid

Fig. 180. *The terrain is fairly bland at this point. Earth Powder is added to the flat surfaces of the mountain.*

Fig. 181. *Very fine scatter is applied over the base of Earth Powder.*

Fig. 182. *To add variety to the colour of the landscape, a second application of scatter is added, this time in a brighter green.*

Summer fine – to be added to the mountain (Fig. 182). The whole landscape is then sprayed with hairspray to help hold the scatters in place.

While the hairspray is still wet, some Noch static grass fibres may be added over the scatters. (The fibres have been applied by hand on the example, not using the Gras-Master applicator.) Most of the fibres will lie flat; this may be the look you are aiming for in mountainous areas (Fig. 183).

It is advisable to allow the glue to dry completely before vacuuming all the loose materials from the scene (Fig. 184).

To hide the join between the bridge and the rock supporting it, apply Raw Grass trimmings (remember that huge supply that was made earlier to keep the groundwork consistent across the layout) to the mountainside where the bridge joins the rock (Fig. 185). First, paint diluted PVA on to the area where

Fig. 183. The flat areas of the mountain top are given a dressing of static grass fibres. Applying them by hand helps them mostly to lie flat, which is the desired effect here.

Fig. 184. There is still much to do on the groundwork but the landscape is taking shape.

Fig. 185. Very finely chopped Raw Grass fibres are used to blend the bridge and the rock together.

Fig. 186. A border of Earth Powder is fixed in place around the edge of the stream.

the fibres are required. You can also add some fibres to the rock below the bridge and along the gravel that borders the stream.

Apply diluted PVA in a narrow bead all the way along the gravel that borders the water's edge and carefully sprinkle Treemendus Earth Powder on top of the glue (Fig. 186). The Earth Powder will soak up the glue and set nice and hard. This border of earth will prevent the resin used for the water in the stream leaking away into the gravel. It also adds a realistic touch to the edge of the stream.

MODELLING THE STREAM

If you want a relatively shallow stream, you can give the whole of the stream bed a layer of Earth Powder, but the aim in the example is to achieve the look of a very deep mountain stream.

In order to give an appearance of depth to the stream, the baseboard – which becomes the bed of the stream – is painted in a dark-coloured paint (Fig. 187). Poster, acrylic or emulsion paints are suitable for this job. The darker the board below the resin, the deeper the water will look. The paint ideally should be applied in strokes that follow the course of the stream; after the resin has been poured into the stream bed, these strokes will look more natural than marks that run across the stream bed.

Of course, sand, gravel, earth or scatter could be fixed to the baseboard and then covered with resin or clear varnish. For more detail on this technique, see Chapter 10.

To add variation to the apparent depth of the water, some of the dark paint is taken off using a dry paintbrush, revealing the lighter colour of the cement undercoat beneath. The paler areas will appear to be shallower than the darker areas – the edges of the stream are more likely to be shallower than the middle (Fig. 188). The paint should be removed in strokes that follow the course of the water. The same effect can be achieved by allowing the first coat of paint to dry and painting over it to produce the effect of shallower areas with paler paint or paints. Again, it is important to follow the course of the stream as you add the paint.

For advice on different techniques for modelling water, see Chapters 7–10. The stream in the example is a simple body of deep running water. The base for the stream is prepared by painting with a dark poster paint and the edges of the stream are sealed with Treemendus Earth Powder and glue.

TREES AND FOLIAGE

Tall conifers are typical of the trees found growing on mountain tops. The trees in the example have

Fig. 187. Painting the bed of the stream in a dark-coloured paint will add depth to it once the 'water' is applied.

Fig. 188. Removing some of the dark paint from the bed and allowing the paler base colour to show through will introduce shallower ledges into the stream.

Fig. 189. If possible, choose trees that suit the environment in which they are to be 'planted'.

wire trunks that have been coated in bark powder to thicken them up slightly. They have also had a wash of paint to give them a more weathered, mossy look.

The trees can be pushed directly into the polystyrene terrain and do not need glue to hold them in place (Fig. 189). Position your trees as you see fit but remember trees can be very useful in hiding certain aspects of the layout from the viewer. Joins in the back scene, roads that go nowhere and entrances to fiddle yards can all be easily hidden by carefully placed trees.

Small clumps of brambles growing in the crevices in the rocks add an extra element to the groundwork. These are made using rubberized horsehair, which has been teased apart, painted and covered in scatter. Tiny bits of bramble may also be added to the landscape (Fig. 190). The underside of each piece

CENTRE LEFT: Fig. 190. Rubberized horsehair brambles are easy to make and add colour and texture to the mountainside.

LEFT: Fig. 191. Adding different species of plants to the groundwork, including laser-cut paper ferns, will create variety.

Tip

Trees are sometimes planted in rows, where they are part of a managed forest, for example, but placing trees in a more random arrangement will add more interest to the landscape. Note how the small conifer in the background adds perspective to the scene.

is coated with PVA glue and placed in position. Use tweezers to manoeuvre the smaller pieces into place.

More interest can be added to the landscape in the form of ferns. Laser-cut plants are very simple to shape and are easily held in place with PVA (Fig. 191). Laser-cut paper ferns from Noch come on a pre-printed, pre-cut sheet and simply require carefully pushing out and positioning.

Noch tufts are placed along the stream, growing in and around the boulders that border it. These are held in place with neat PVA (Fig. 192). Tufts are also added around the sides of the stream and will eventually be standing in the water itself.

Avoid the temptation to add too many plants, which can often spoil the effect.

SNOW

Snow is not often seen on UK layouts as UK railway modellers tend to model summertime, when everything in their home country is lush and often very green.

A sprinkling of snow may be added to the scene using Treemendus Snow. First, cover tracks with masking tape or narrow strips of paper to avoid getting glue and snow on to the track and into point mechanisms. Take some PVA glue and dilute it by

Fig. 192. Clumps of tall reeds can be added to the edge of the stream and the surrounding scree slope.

Fig. 193. A light covering of snow really adds to the atmosphere of the mountain top.

Fig. 194. Thick drifts of snow are easy to create and can look very realistic.

approximately 4 parts water to 1 part glue. This is best mixed in a bottle which has an atomizer-type spray for its lid. Add a drop of washing-up liquid and shake it well to mix the three components together.

Using the atomizer, spray the glue on to the area where you want the snow to appear. It may be best to work on small sections at a time; spraying on the glue then applying the snow. To apply the snow, take small pinches of it between your thumb and forefinger and sprinkle it on to the wet glue. The depth of the snow can be controlled by adding more for a thicker covering and less for a lighter covering, or where it has started to thaw. If you do not have an atomizer bottle you can apply the diluted glue to the groundwork using a paintbrush. Try to keep the glue to the area where you want the snow and dab up any dribbles with a small lint-free cloth.

When the required coverage of snow has been achieved (Fig. 193), spray the groundwork with hairspray. Avoid getting any snow stuck to the bed of the stream.

For thicker drifts of snow, apply the snow to the groundwork, using a soft paintbrush to brush it into the desired position, then take your hairspray and, from a distance far enough away not to move it, give it a good soaking. Next, lightly spray the drift with the PVA mixture and another light application of hairspray. This will dry and set into a very durable drift of snow (Fig. 194). Again, if you do not have an atomizer, then use a soft paintbrush and allow the diluted glue to drip from the brush and into the snow, taking care not to disturb it.

The product used for the water is Solid Water, from Deluxe Materials. This is a two-part resin that, when mixed together, sets to produce a wonderfully clear water effect. Follow the instructions on the box carefully – in this case 2 parts resin to 1 part hardener (Fig. 195).

The resin mixture is poured on to the bed of the stream and can be worked into small recesses along the stream and around plants growing along the water's edge using the spatula supplied or a wooden skewer (Fig. 196). A 1–2mm layer is enough to create the illusion of deep water.

THE COMPLETED DIORAMA

The layout represents a little slice of a mountainous region, where a bridge crosses over a deep body of water. A mountain stream appears from the rear of the landscape and makes its way towards the front of the scene. Tall conifers add to the realism of the environment and a sprinkling of snow gives the impression that the landscape is at a high altitude.

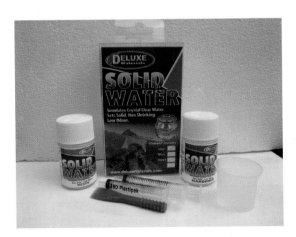

Fig. 195. Always read the instructions carefully before preparing resins and be careful when using them.

Fig. 196. Two-part resins stay workable for some time and can be dragged into place with a wooden skewer.

Fig. 197. A small section of mountain railway with a light covering of snow. The bridge that carries trains over the ravine is suitably weathered and the water below the bridge has realistic movement to its surface.

SUMMARY

Polystyrene is a very useful, lightweight material and very suitable when it comes to making tall mountains, as it is easy to carve and shape. The addition of cork granules to the cement coating of the polystyrene gives a textural look to the rock that is different from that produced by some of the other methods. The surface of the rock was given a thin wash with diluted emulsion paint but dry brushing would give very good results too. Minimal amounts of scatter were used to add greenery to the landscape and a light sprinkling of snow, which is optional, adds another element to the landscape.

Fig. 198. A short passenger train approaches a small timber bridge on its way through rugged scenery as late spring snow melts away under the welcome sunshine.

CHAPTER SEVEN

WATERFALLS

Fig. 199. Waterfalls in nature range from small trickles to huge torrents, which can create lots of white water and spray.

Materials

- Ply board
- Kingspan
- Cement
- PVA glue
- Scenic modelling materials
- Paints/weathering powders

Tools

- Steel rule
- Jigsaw
- Sandpaper
- Scalpel/Stanley knife
- Large paintbrush
- Small firm paintbrushes

Through the effects of gravity, water naturally makes its way downhill towards lower ground. There are certain techniques that may be used to model streams as they find their way downhill, cutting their way through the landscape, forming waterfalls and white water. The advice here moves downhill from the deep flowing mountain stream to a more dynamic body of water.

A waterfall is formed by water, often from a river or stream, dropping from a higher to a lower point. Sometimes, it is made up from a series of smaller waterfalls (as here) but sometimes the water falls in a single drop from a great height, making a very dramatic feature in the landscape. The streams that form waterfalls can eventually join up with other streams to form a larger body of water, such as a river or an inland lake. One of the most dramatic waterfalls is the Kinder Scout downfall in the Peak District National Park in Derbyshire, where a strong south-westerly wind can make the water blow up instead of down!

In the example, the deep channels have been a long time in the making and the steep walls have been carved out by the action of flowing water for many years. Moss and other plant life cling to the rock walls that edge it.

The motion of the water needs to be captured in order to add some movement to the scene. White-water foam builds up at the bottom of the waterfall and debris from winters past gathers around the rocks in this autumn scene. A fallen tree spans the gap, creating a natural bridge from one side of the chasm to the other.

The following method of creating the effect of moving water can be used to replicate vast falls of water on multiple levels, or a small step in what is no more than a stream running its course downhill.

PLANNING AND PREPARATION

Many of the features created when modelling railway layouts can easily be seamlessly blended together. A waterfall feature is no exception. Whether you are using or have used chicken wire, polystyrene, Kingspan or card and newspaper, or a mixture of all four methods, to shape your landscape, it is a simple task to create a space where the waterfall or a series of waterfalls can be placed. Simply cut out a section of the landscape and create a channel in which to build a rocky gorge for the water to fall down.

If the early stages of the terrain are planned correctly, the hard landscaping on either side of the waterfall can be boxed off, leaving a neat void in between. A box can be made to fit snugly inside the void, allowing the waterfall section to be constructed away from the layout and then slipped into place after it is built (Fig. 200). This method can be applied to other features on the landscape, such as a copse of trees, for example, which is much easier to fix to a section of polystyrene or Kingspan than into a chicken-wire frame. This method is particularly useful for areas of the layout that may be difficult to reach.

Once the landscape feature – for example, the waterfall – has been positioned on the layout, it is just a simple matter of blending the edges of the 'box' into the landscape either side of it using the various methods and materials.

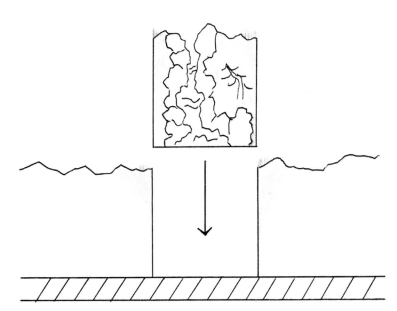

Fig. 200. Small sections of scenery can be made away from the layout and dropped into place once they are complete.

Fig. 201. A simple frame that will contain the waterfall can be made using a number of materials.

Fig. 202. Kingspan pieces are the main material used for the rock surrounding the waterfall. Being lightweight and easy to cut, it is ideal for such applications.

Measure, mark and cut the frame that will house the waterfall. In the example, ply board is used for the base of the frame and polystyrene sheet for the back and sides, but thick card or a similar light-weight sheet material will work just as well. Be sure to shape the slope of the polystyrene on either side of the waterfall feature to mirror the terrain on the main layout, so, once it has been slipped into posi-tion on the layout, the joins will be less obvious. The sides and back of the frame can be glued in place, using either PVA or grab adhesive, and left to dry (Fig. 201).

CONSTRUCTION

The rocks over which the water flows, creating the waterfall, are made using Kingspan (see Chapter 5), this time coated in a cement mixture (see Chapter 2). Take the block of Kingspan and hold it on a flat surface with one hand. With a sharp knife, roughly chop chunks in a variety of sizes and shapes – some thick blocks and thin slithers give plenty of scope when it comes to putting the pieces together. Snapping some pieces off the sheet by hand can also result in realistic texture to the chunks (Fig. 202).

Picture in your mind how wide the waterfall should be, and how deep you want the drops in the waterfall to be, and chop accordingly. There is no need to be too accurate at this stage as the blocks will be refined as the waterfall is constructed. It is recommended that you make more than you actu-ally need as this gives more scope when it comes to arranging them.

Start to build the waterfall feature by arranging pieces of Kingspan at the point where the waterfall ends on the layout (Fig. 203). This is where the last fall becomes a pool of water and a flowing stream again. Adding this feature before the upper parts of the waterfall ensures that the waterfall ends in the correct place on the layout.

This step is important and reference to photo-graphs of waterfalls may help you here.

The first stage in creating the falls is to construct a number of steps, which get higher as they get further back, in other words, further up the water-fall. Remember that waterfalls do not necessarily fall straight down slopes as they work their way around the rocks; indeed, your model scenery will have more character if the waterfall has kinks in it. Once the drops, over which the water falls, are in position (Fig. 204) they may be held in place with grab adhesive.

The rear of the polystyrene frame also has a section cut away where the waterfall joins the landscape.

It is best to start the positioning of the rock walls around the waterfall at the bottom of the falls. Take

Fig. 203. Start building your waterfall by positioning the Kingspan at the bottom of the structure.

Fig. 204. The height of the falls is dictated by the size of the blocks used to fashion the steps in it.

some of the small pieces of Kingspan and arrange them in such a way that they look natural and realistic (Fig. 205). The great thing about using Kingspan for this type of work is that it is very easy to shape into pieces that are useful for constructing the falls and the walls around them, and for filling small gaps as you work your way around the waterfall. Continue adding further pieces, working your way uphill as you go, creating a channel for the water to run through.

> **Tip**
>
> It is also worth considering disguising the point at which the waterfall enters the landscape, either by using rocky outcrops or a mass of trees or foliage. This avoids the impression of a waterfall coming straight out from the back scene.

Fig. 205. Create a channel for the water to run down as you add more Kingspan to the sides of the falls.

Fig. 206. The main structure of the waterfall is in place.

Fig. 207. If required, the surface of the rock can be carved to add more detail.

Fig. 208. The cement coat has been allowed to dry – all the tiny gaps are now sealed and watertight.

Another feature of real waterfalls is plunge pools – deep pools of water in the rock at the bottom of drops, formed by the action of the water eroding the rock. These can be created by carving out a little hollow at the foot of the falls, not too deep – 5–10mm will suffice.

As more Kingspan pieces are added to the groundwork, the feature will begin to take shape. The channel is purposely made slightly narrower the further up the slope it gets (Fig. 206), adding a touch of perspective to the landscape. Grab adhesive or PVA glue is used to hold all the Kingspan in place. Allow the structure to dry.

The polystyrene sheet that forms the back and sides of the frame is shaped using a sharp carving knife to slope down towards the rocks surrounding the waterfall.

To add more detail to the surface of the Kingspan, some of it is carved using a sharp blade (Fig. 207). In nature some rock faces are smoother than others, especially where the effect of running water has played a part in their history, and it is very much a personal choice as to the overall texture of the rocks and how many cracks and crevices appear in yours.

To enhance the look of the rock and to help seal any gaps that may be present in and around the floor of the waterfall, a thin coat of cement mixed with diluted PVA is applied to the gaps and all over the surface of the Kingspan. Make sure this seals even the tiniest of gaps, as it is this coating that will stop the Scenic Water, which is added at a later stage, from seeping away.

A hard shell of flat terrain is added to either side of the waterfall, sitting flush with the terrain on either

Fig. 209. Boulders and rocks can be added to the floor of the waterfall if required. Some waterfalls have very few, whilst others can be filled with them.

Fig. 210. Integrating some of the rock used on the waterfall into the surrounding landscape helps it to fit more naturally into the scenery.

side when the frame is put in position on the layout. It is made from strips of paper coated with PVA glue laid over screwed-up newspaper, then given a thin coat of the cement mixture to help fill any of the gaps between the rocks and the paper. The coating is then allowed to dry (Fig. 208).

Large boulders and small rocks will often be found in the middle of the course of a waterfall. These rocks often fall from the ground surrounding the waterfall as the softer rock and earth around it are washed away. To add a couple of large boulders to the floor of the waterfall (Fig. 209), take pieces of Kingspan coated with the cement mixture and fix them in place with a spot of PVA glue.

The realism of features such as waterfalls, quarries and railway cuttings can be enhanced if some of the rock used in their creation is also added nearby on the landscape, visually gelling the areas of groundwork together. For example (Fig. 210), Kingspan boulders may be glued to the terrain on the right-hand side of the waterfall. These can be positioned to overlap the join between this section and the static sections of terrain on the layout. It is good practice at this point to make a few extra boulders, which can be worked into the surrounding landscape and placed in the bottom of the channel where the water runs.

PAINTING, WEATHERING AND DETAILING

When the cement coating has dried, the texture of the rock can be highlighted by dry brushing on assorted tones of paint. This will add to the realism of the waterfall. The first coat is black emulsion paint with a small dab of white emulsion added to it to lighten it a touch. The mix is then diluted (1 part paint to 6 parts water) and the whole surface of the rock can be painted with it. This dark mix of paint is used to darken all the cracks and crevices among the rocks. Allow this coat of paint to dry before adding lighter tones to the surface.

The lighter shades, as before, will be dry brushed. Again, matt white emulsion paint is used as the base colour for the mixes and again three different shades are mixed, based on the same paint colours. These mixes can be blended at random throughout the painting process:

- Mix 1: 8 parts matt white; 3 parts yellow; 2 parts black.
- Mix 2: 8 parts matt white; 2 parts yellow; 1 part black.
- Mix 3: 10 parts matt white; 1 part yellow; 0.5 part black.

For best results when dry brushing it is important to allow each tone of paint to dry before applying the next, lighter tone. When dry brushing, dip the tips of the bristles of a firm brush into the paint. Next, wipe the tip of the bristles on a dry cloth or tissue to remove most of the paint, and, using the bristle tips only, just catch the edges and any tiny protrusions of the rock formations. This gives a great impression of weathered rock (Fig. 211).

Avoid using pure black or white on the rock as this may look unrealistic. Leaving the undersides of any overhangs dark is an effective way of introducing shadows to the waterfall. It is always recommended that you paint a test piece first, especially if dry brushing is a technique that you have not used before. The test piece should be left to dry to see if the colour of rock you want has been achieved. For more in-depth advice on dry brushing, see Chapter 2.

Fig. 211. Dry brushing with a range of paints brings out all the surface detail present on the rocks.

Fig. 212. Weathering the rock adds to the realism of the scene. Moss is also a common sight growing around such constantly damp places.

Fig. 213. A hand-made windswept tree adds to the ruggedness of the landscape. Wire armatures can be shaped to suit any situation.

Fig. 214. Forest Floor scatter from Treemendus is added to all the ledges and flat areas around the waterfall.

Obviously, the rocks surrounding a waterfall can be wet all the time and this allows algae and mosses to proliferate on their surface. This effect can be represented by adding weathering pigments (Fig. 212). Treemendus Spring scatter fine may also be added to some of the rocks surrounding the water, fixed in place with Scenefix glue and a light spray of hairspray.

For a striking feature, a slightly windswept tree can be introduced to the edge of the chasm (Fig. 213), the bends in its trunk echoing the bends of the waterfall. The tree is a hand-made wire armature coated with Bark Powder. It is made with a little planting pin, which can be pushed directly into the groundwork and, if necessary, held in place with glue. Its root system is blended into the existing surface using the cement mixture.

As with many of the techniques described for creating ground cover, scatters and scenic modelling

Autumn colours

To add some variety to the range of layouts described here, this scene is set firmly in the midst of autumn. Obviously, you will not build your waterfall using autumnal colours if the rest of your scenics are based on summer colours, but autumn colours can be very effective and are often overlooked. Oranges, yellows and washed-out greens look great together and complement the dark greens of conifers.

Fig. 215. Small roots and twigs are added to the scene, both in and around the waterfall.

Fig. 216. Raw Grass 'moss' added to the rocks not only looks very realistic but is also useful for filling any unrealistic-looking gaps.

materials are applied in layers. Treemendus Forest Floor is applied to the groundwork on and around the waterfall, sprinkled on a layer of Scenefix glue (Fig. 214). As its name implies, Forest Floor contains all the detritus found on the ground underneath trees and bushes and in areas such as this, where it has been blown by the wind and come to rest on the ledges around the waterfall.

Another useful part of the Forest Floor material is the tiny roots and twigs included in the bag. These can be fixed in place on the bed of the stream and among the cracks and crevices along the side of the waterfall (Fig. 215). This gives the impression of branches that have been carried there by the water or fallen from the tree above the chasm. A spot of glue will help hold them in place.

Raw Grass fibres are useful for enhancing the walls of the waterfall. A thin coat of Scenefix glue on the rocky ledges is enough to hold them in place and they are then worked into place with a wooden skewer (Fig. 216).

GO WITH THE FLOW

There are a number of steps to follow when introducing the Scenic Water into the landscape. All the materials used in the production of the water here are from Deluxe Materials.

Drape scenic fibres over the edges of the falls and trim with scissors to a length slightly longer than the falls. Apply PVA glue to the edge of the fall with a paintbrush and push the fibres into the glue, ensuring that they are firmly attached (Fig. 217). The more fibres you use, the thicker the fall of water will appear. Fibres can also be used to create white water around the rocks, boulders and branches in and around the waterfall if necessary.

Spray the fibres with hairspray to make them a little more rigid, then mix a little white acrylic paint with some pre-prepared Scenic Water and carefully apply it with a paintbrush on to the fibres. The fibres will set hard and form a rigid frame for the falling water (Fig. 218). Remove with scissors any fibres that look too thick and spoil the look of the water.

Fig. 217. Scenic fibres are added to the edges of the rocks and held in place with PVA glue.

Fig. 218. Hairspray helps to keep the fibres rigid.

Prepare the Scenic Water according to the instructions and, whilst it is still fluid, pour it into the 'plunge pools' at the bottom of each of the falls. The bottoms of the plunge pools are painted using very dark paint so that, when the Scenic Water has dried, they will appear to be very deep.

Solid Water, a two-part resin, is mixed according to the manufacturer's instructions and poured into the bed of the waterfall, over the front of the scenic fibres, and worked around all the rocks and boulders on the bed (Fig. 219). Be sure to visualize how the water would move through the structure and position the fibres accordingly.

The movement of the water causes splashing and it is effective to add some wetness to the rock surrounding the water. Taking a small amount of Solid Water from the bottom of your mixing pot, paint it with a stiff paintbrush on to the areas around the rock where you would expect to see splashing (Fig. 220). If you have any hollows on your surrounding

Fig. 219. A two-part resin is mixed and poured into the waterfall and on to the fibres attached to the rocks.

Fig. 220. Adding some resin to the rock walls around the waterfall adds to the illusion of splashing and movement of the water.

rock, try adding a small amount of the Solid Water into them to create small pockets of water among the mossy rocks. Allow the Solid Water to dry.

To add more movement to the surface of the water, take some Making Waves product and using a small paintbrush apply it to the surface of the water already present in the waterfall. Use a stippling action to create small waves, swirls and splashes on the surface of the water. Making Waves is white when applied but dries to a clear finish (Fig. 221).

Making Waves can be used for small waterfalls without the need to use scenic fibres.

To add to the effect of even more movement in the water, mix a little Making Waves with a spot of white emulsion paint (acrylic paint will work just as well) and use a stiff, short-bristled brush to apply it on and around the rocks, boulders and walls of the waterfall (Fig. 222). Be aware that this process leads the product to dry white and not clear, as it does in the previous step, so take care where you put it and how much you use. In truth there is no right or wrong as some waterfalls have very little white water while others are full of spray and froth.

> **Tip**
>
> Do make sure you have sealed the bed of the waterfall and all the gaps in the surrounding walls with either a cement/PVA mix, as here, or with a clear varnish before pouring on any of the water materials. If you fail to do this, the resin will find any gaps and seep away.

Fig. 221. The Making Waves product is applied to create texture and movement to the surface of the water. Although it is applied as a white gel, it dries clear.

Fig. 222. Applying another layer of Making Waves, this time with white paint mixed in with it, adds to the white water effect.

DETAILING THE GROUNDWORK

To help with the blending in of the waterfall feature with the terrain on either side of it on the layout, the groundwork around the rocks surrounding the waterfall needs some attention. Carefully paint dilute PVA around the rocks using a small paintbrush on to which Treemendus Earth Powder is sprinkled. Finely chopped Raw Grass fibres are then applied around

Fig. 223. Small gaps around the base of rocks can be filled using finely chopped Raw Grass fibres, fixed in place using diluted PVA glue.

the bases of the rocks and worked into place with a wooden skewer (Fig. 223).

Add taller tufts of Raw Grass around the rocks on either side of the waterfall. To achieve this effect, take a sheet of Raw Grass material and colour it using Sap Green acrylic paint – dilute the paint (4 parts water to 1 part paint) and rub it into the fibres by hand, making sure the paint is worked well into the sheet. It may be useful to add a small dab of neat Sap Green paint to a section of the sheet and rub this in too. Other small areas of the sheet may be coloured with a variety of different-coloured paints, to give a sheet of material that has various tones of fibres and can be used as a palette to add lots of variation to the groundwork around the waterfall.

To fix the tufts in place, it is important to use neat PVA or a glue of similar viscosity. The tufts are trimmed from the sheet using sharp scissors and their flat bottoms are dipped in the thick glue and carefully placed on to the groundwork (Fig. 224). Having a palette of different but complementary colours of tufts will allow you to add lots of character to the landscape.

The tufts can be blended in with the surrounding landscape on either side of the waterfall once it is in position on the layout. Static grass fibres can be

Fig. 224. Small tufts of weeds are easy to create, using Raw Grass fibres held in place on the groundwork with neat PVA glue.

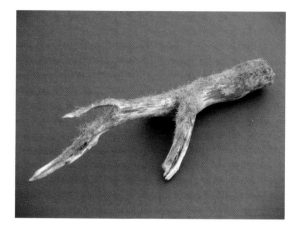

Fig. 225. *Pieces of natural wood can be used to great effect. This piece has been given a layer of moss and resembles an old fallen tree trunk.*

Fig. 226. *Small bushes and shrubs can be created using tiny pieces of Seamoss covered with autumnal-coloured scatters. These are ready to fix into the ground around the waterfall.*

used around the rocks instead, or as well, if the surrounding landscape is to be dressed with static grass.

To complement the windswept tree on the edge of the waterfall a fallen tree is placed across the gap that spans the waterfall (Fig. 225). This tree is actually a piece of naturally weathered branch which has been enhanced with weathering pigments to match the windswept tree in appearance. A light covering

of Raw Grass trimmings is applied to the upper side of it, to represent the moss that grows on fallen trees such as this. The pre-coloured Raw Grass (painted in the previous step) is trimmed with scissors into very fine, tiny fibres. The top of the fallen tree is coated with diluted PVA and the fibres are worked into the glue. It is best to do this away from the waterfall and fix it in place once it has dried.

Fig. 227. *The small bushes blend in well with the rest of the groundwork.*

Fig. 228. A solitary figure shows the scale of the scene.

Seamoss is a natural product that is useful for creating small shrubs and bushes. It lends itself perfectly to autumn and winter scenes where its fine 'branches' can be appreciated because only a minimal amount of foliage is added to them. Choose suitably sized pieces of Seamoss and carefully remove any leaves that may be present on the stalks. Seamoss is generally an unrealistic yellowish colour naturally and a spray of paint, in this instance a mid-brown,

will give it a more pleasing bark colour. A dry brush of white paint may be given to mimic young silver birch. The Seamoss is then sprayed with hairspray and autumnal-coloured scatters are applied sparingly (Fig. 226). On the example, Treemendus Autumn Orange, Autumn Yellow and Late Summer fine scatters are applied to the bushes. To fix the scatters permanently, spray the Seamoss with Scenefix glue.

The Seamoss shrubs and bushes are fixed into the groundwork using a spot of superglue. A small hole may be created in the Kingspan into which the stalk of the Seamoss can be pushed.

A single figure is sometimes just enough to show the scale of model scenery to the best effect (Fig. 228).

THE COMPLETED DIORAMA

In the completed layout (Fig. 229), the movement of the water is very apparent as it makes its way downhill over the rocky features. Debris from the passing of the seasons has collected in the bottom of the falls and on ledges around the chasm. Moss is prolific and is a colourful addition to the rock. The autumn colours of the foliage are subtle but help to capture this little slice of countryside well. It is quite unusual for British railway modellers to set a layout in autumn, but it can be extremely effective.

Fig. 229. Everything in the scene blends together in perfect harmony. The fallen tree makes an interesting feature to the waterfall.

SUMMARY

Waterfalls do not have to be made in small scenic sections away from the layout but it can help in the construction of such scenic features, especially if space around its position on the layout is restricted. Although there are other ways of constructing rock formations like this, Kingspan lends itself well to the job.

Waterfalls are fairly common in the British countryside through which trains travel. They make an excellent feature on any model railway and do not take up any extra space. If you are building hills or even small slopes on your layout it is well worth thinking about even a small water feature, always taking into consideration where the stream flows from the bottom of the waterfall in relation to the rest of your layout.

Fig. 230. Misty early morning in the valleys. The waterfall makes a dramatic backdrop to the foreground and the trains running in front of it.

CHAPTER EIGHT

SLOW-FLOWING STREAMS

Fig. 231. A typical slow-flowing polluted stream.

Materials

- Kingspan
- Finishing plaster or cement
- PVA glue/superglue
- Corrugated card
- Plastic strip
- Wire
- Scenic modelling materials
- Paints/weathering powders

Tools

- Steel rule
- Scalpel/Stanley knife
- Sandpaper
- Large paintbrush

The slow-flowing, shallow stream is a feature of the flatter landscape that is found a little further downstream from the mountain stream and waterfall. In the example, it runs around the outskirts of an industrial area and the effects of pollution can be seen in the water and its surroundings. Streams flow naturally along fixed routes formed by a channel cut into rock or ground. Brooks and rivers can also be made using the following methods.

Streams and brooks can be found running through all sorts of places, including industrial estates, the edges of busy roads and around the outskirts of housing estates. Such streams can be anything but fresh and clean.

The stream in the example is set in a more urban setting and various techniques may be used to create a slow-flowing gently meandering stream affected by the pollution associated with industry. The stream's course is determined by what lies underneath the ground – as the water cuts into the sub-surface and meets rock, the stream gently bends. A railway viaduct dominates the landscape.

PLANNING

There are two ways to introduce a stream into your layout. The first way is to cut away a thin section of baseboard and use this as the channel in which the stream runs. This channel needs to be wider than the stream's final width because it will have to house the banks and the bed of the stream (Fig. 232). Small girder bridges taking trains over streams like this look great and can be a nice feature in their own right.

Another way to introduce a stream is to gradually build up the height of the baseboard, creating a channel through which the stream can flow (Fig. 233). This way you will be using the original level of the baseboard as the bed of the stream. If this is done with some thought it will blend well into the scenery, as opposed to looking like it has been added as an

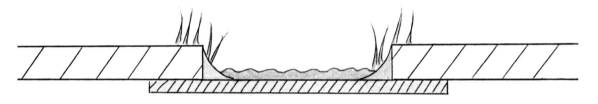

Fig. 232. Line drawing showing a cut-out section of baseboard; this creates a sunken stream bed.

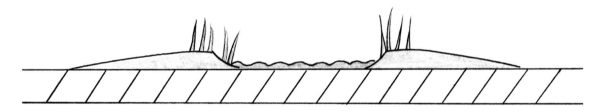

Fig. 233. Line drawing showing built-up stream banks; the baseboard is used for the water level.

Creating split-level scenery

The idea in the example is that the stream is a feature below the main baseboard level, with the track on the viaduct being at the level of the main baseboard.

Creating a drop in baseboard levels is a fairly simple task. If your boards are already built, use a jigsaw to cut a section wide enough to fit the feature, whether this is a viaduct, bridge or steep grassy embankment. Strengthen the sawn edges with a timber framework and measure them to the desired depth of the drop in the scenery. The resulting gap can be spanned by a piece of ply board attached to the lower sides of the timber supports.

If your baseboards are yet to be constructed, plan for features such as this before building begins. Baseboards built in rooms with chimney breasts can use this design to advantage. The boards that end on either side of the chimney breast can be joined by a piece of board set lower than the baseboards on either side, for example. A viaduct or bridge can be incorporated into the design, sat on the lower level board running in front of the chimney breast.

Split-level model railways, even with the smallest difference in baseboard levels, are always so much more interesting and more natural-looking than models presented on a flat surface.

Fig. 234. The stream runs beneath an old weathered viaduct. The basic terrain has been shaped.

afterthought. That said, it is not unusual to see the banks of small streams purposely built up where they flow through industrial and public areas, to deal with the event of high water levels.

The second option is a simpler way to introduce a stream to your layout as it avoids the removal of any of the baseboard. It may be the best solution for adding a stream that does not interfere with the track.

A third option is to paint the bed of the stream directly on to the baseboard and either cover it with acetate or apply varnish over it. The edges of the stream are then added using scenic modelling materials.

CONSTRUCTION

The basic terrain is formed using the familiar materials and techniques. The steep slopes on either side of the stream are created from Kingspan (or Styrofoam or polystyrene) by carving it with a sharp knife. They are shaped to fit the space available and then fixed with grab adhesive. Here, the base used is a piece of Kingspan, but ply would be more suited to a railway

layout, with a piece of Kingspan glued to the top of it. The stream is cut out of the base with a sharp knife, and characteristic bends and turns are incorporated into the watercourse.

A small railway viaduct at the rear of the scene (the track on the viaduct would be at the main base-board level) is painted and weathered to suit its eventual surroundings, using a mix of AK Interactive enamels and pigments. It will be refined further at a later step. The efflorescence (white streaking) on the brickwork of the viaduct is common on such structures and is easily modelled. Take a spot of white paint on a very fine brush and remove most of it on

Fig. 235. Details are carved out of the Kingspan, in this case the paths either side of the stream.

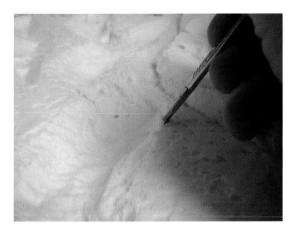

Fig. 236. The banks of the stream are refined by carving them at realistic angles.

Fig. 237. A thin plaster shell is applied over the Kingspan. This enables you to create a level bed to the stream and seal any gaps present in it.

a cloth so that only a little remains on the bristles. Using downward vertical strokes, run the brush over the brickwork creating tiny streaks (Fig. 234).

The shape of the Kingspan is refined with a sharp blade, which cuts through it easily. It should be shaped to look natural from all angles. Cut a pathway from the Kingspan using a sharp scalpel (Fig. 235). Paths like this are generally fairly uneven so try to make yours rise up and down, as opposed to being clinically flat. The path goes beneath the viaduct and out of sight, while a path on the other side of the stream goes up towards the viaduct.

The banks of the stream are refined to look more natural. Use a sharp blade to shape the bank and to make some areas of it wider than others. Cut the bank away at both shallow and steep angles; shallow angles look better on the outsides of the bends while steeper banks look better on the insides of the bends (Fig. 236). The Kingspan will be covered by a plaster coating, so you need not be too concerned about accuracy at this stage.

Once you are happy with the shape of the terrain and the detailing that has been added to it, it can be sealed using either a cement or plaster-based coating. On the example, finishing plaster is applied to the Kingspan using a butter knife (Fig. 237). Fill any unwanted gaps that may be present around features

on your landscape – for example, the viaduct – and be sure to seal the bed of the stream to avoid any of the Scenic Water leaking out.

Streams created in this way need not be very deep. If the channel you have carved will require unnecessarily large volumes of Scenic Water (and it probably will, in all fairness), now is a good time to raise the bed of the stream using the plaster to make it shallower. Try to keep it fairly flat by skimming over it with a knife, or a piece of plastic or card.

A short length of plastic pipe has been added to the bank on the left-hand side to act as an overflow into the stream. To the rear of the scene a culvert adds a second flow of water into the stream; a wider pipe with a steel grille has been added into the bank just under the viaduct.

FENCING

Although there is a wide choice of quality ready-made fencing available to railway modellers, it is always useful to be able to make your own, especially if you only need a short length for a specific place. Corrugated-iron and wooden-planked fences can be found around the perimeter of both industrial and rural properties and will be suited to most regions and eras.

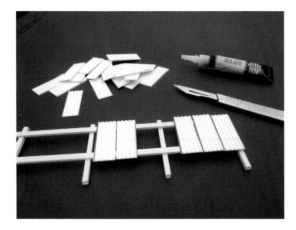

Fig. 238. Corrugated card and plastic strips make very good fences. Fences like these are very common and are simple to create.

CORRUGATED-IRON FENCES

Corrugated-iron sheets do vary in size, but one common dimension is approximately 3 x 9ft (90 x 270cm), which equates to 12mm by 36mm in 1:76. Carefully measure and mark either corrugated cardboard (as in the example) or embossed plastic sheet. Using a very sharp blade, carefully cut out the number of 12 x 36mm pieces you will need for the length of fencing required and put these to one side.

Plastic strips are used to create a frame on which to fix the corrugated sheets. Make the vertical posts

longer than the corrugated panels as this will help when it comes to fixing the fence into the ground-work. Construct the framework – the posts are 46mm in height and the space between the two horizontal strips is 25mm – with the lower strip positioned 15mm from the bottom of the posts. Lay the frame on a flat surface with the horizontal strips uppermost. Use superglue to fix the corrugated sheets to the frame, positioning the bottom of the panels approximately 10mm up from the bottom of the posts.

The effect of separate panels can be highlighted if the corrugated card is attached slightly informally. One option is to leave one or more gaps the same width as the panels – in this case 12mm – when attaching them (Fig. 238). To add a little variety to a corrugated iron fence, it is a nice touch to give the impression that one or more of the panels has been replaced with newer, more shiny ones. To do this, cut a piece of ordinary household silver foil to twice the width of the panels on your fence. Spray the panel using a spray adhesive or coat it in a very thin coat of PVA applied with a brush. Next, take the silver foil and carefully work it into the grooves of the corrugated card using a soft sponge or a cleaning bud (Fig. 239). Apply glue to the back of the card and fold the foil around the back, then put it to one side to dry.

Of course, if you want a new-looking fence the whole length can be given the same treatment. More

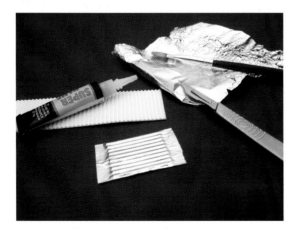

Fig. 239. New-looking panels add character to the old fence.

Fig. 240. Undercoating the fence panels in a bright colour adds to the final appearance of the fence.

Fig. 241. Black paint is painted over the first coat. The undercoat is purposely allowed to show through.

simply, you can spray the panels with silver aerosol paint.

The corrugated-iron fence can be painted any colour you choose. Undercoating it with one or more colours and then applying a further coat of a different colour can give the impression of a fence that has been painted more than once and has started to flake.

To achieve the effect of an old weathered fence, spray with a grey primer, allow it to dry and then give the panels a coat of a coloured paint. A second, rough coat is then applied using an aqua green emulsion paint. This need not be applied evenly – leaving some of the grey undercoat showing through will only add to the desired effect (Fig. 240).

When the emulsion paint has dried, a top coat of matt black emulsion can be added, using a brush and purposely applied in a manner that allows the coats underneath to show through. Let the top coat of paint dry completely.

To highlight the corrugation of the fence panels, take a piece of very fine sandpaper and lightly sand the corrugated card horizontally across the panels. This will take a tiny amount of paint off and allow the undercoat or card to show through (Fig. 241).

Another very effective way of reproducing chipped and flaking paint is to paint the fence as described in the previous step and allow it to dry. Take a small paintbrush and lightly dampen little patches of the fence where you would like to see the undercoat colour showing through once your final coat of paint is on. Sprinkle a little salt (sea salt is best, due to its irregular sized grains) on to the dampened area. The grains will be held in place as the water on them

dries. Next paint the fence using an airbrush or aerosol – make sure you keep the device far enough from the fence, so you do not blow the grains away. When the top coat of paint dries, the salt can be removed using a soft brush, leaving the undercoat showing through the top coat. This will give the very convincing effect of chippings and flaking.

To finish the detailing of the corrugated-iron fence and to add to its weathered state, AK Interactive rust pigments and enamels have been used to give a

Fig. 242. Rust is added to the old panels on the fence, and the newer panels. Details like these can really enhance a simple feature such as a fence.

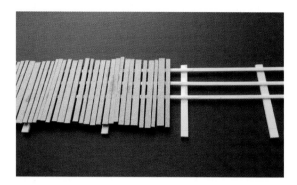

Fig. 243. Wooden-planked fencing is very easy to make. Here, 1mm thick card strips are glued to a plastic frame.

Fig. 244. The appearance of fences like this can be enhanced by the careful use of painting techniques. Missing planks and planks that have been replaced add to the appearance of the fence.

Fig. 245. Green algae gives the fence a realistic finish.

pleasing aged look. The shiny panels are then glued in place and are weathered with only a light dressing of rust paint (Fig. 242).

Some of the corners of the older panels are bent over to imply damage to the fence – another example of a tiny detail that adds to the overall effect of an old and weathered fence.

WOODEN-PLANK FENCING

Wooden-plank fencing is produced in a very similar way to corrugated-iron fencing. Measure and cut thin strips of plastic, card or real wood such as basswood or balsa. On the example, plastic strips are used for the frame and very thin card for the planks on the fencing.

Make the framework by cutting posts that are longer than the height of the finished fence. This will mean that they can be fixed securely into the groundwork. To add variation to your layout, make your wooden fencing a little lower (or higher) than the corrugated-iron card. This time, when gluing the vertical strips of plastic to the frame, leave small gaps between them. This adds to the character of the fencing and allows a hint of what is behind the fence to show through (Fig. 243). Random widths of card representing the planks of the fence will add to the rural surroundings.

A coat of acrylic paint is applied to the wooden fence to represent a basic wood colour. This coat is left to dry completely and then a second coat of paint is applied, this time a thin coat of slightly off-white emulsion paint. This coat is also allowed to dry thoroughly. To weather the fence and add an aged look to it, take some very fine sandpaper and lightly rub at the surface of the emulsion, removing some of it and exposing the wood coat of paint below it (Fig. 244).

Next, AK Interactive light and dark grime enamels give the fence a pleasing aged look. Green slime and algae tend to grow around the bottom of walls and fences, so giving these areas a more condensed covering of pigments can add to their realism. As with the corrugated-iron fence some of the planks on the wooden fence can be left clear of emulsion paint, resulting in the appearance of newer, replacement planks (Fig. 245).

Fig. 246. It is important to fix the fencing securely into the groundwork, either now or at a later stage.

Emulsion paints are useful for finishing fences like these because they lend themselves perfectly to a rustic, weathered finish. For neater, more refined fences, acrylic or enamel paints are recommended.

This type of fencing is completely flexible, which may be useful when adding it to your landscape.

Both the corrugated-iron fencing and wooden-plank fencing can be held in place by adding a spot of glue on the bottom of each post (Fig. 246). You may prefer to mark out the position of the posts on the landscape and then fix the fences in place at a later stage.

Fig. 247. The old goods yard sidings are protected by similarly old fences. The effectiveness of these types of fencing can be seen here and they are well worth taking the time to create.

Fig. 248. Treemendus Earth Powder gives the bed of the stream a realistic look. The powder can also be useful in levelling out any little dips in the stream.

Fig. 249. The paths and any other areas of earth are added to the landscape. The paths are given a little texture to their surface in the form of weathered ballast.

DETAILING

The first step of detailing the stream is to cover its bed in a suitable coating of paint or a textured surface. This could be gravel, sand, large rocks or pebbles, depending on the type of landscape being portrayed. Diluted PVA glue is painted on to and around the bed of the stream and Treemendus Earth Powder is sprinkled over it. To help hold it in place, give it a spray with hairspray, from a distance that will not blow the powder away (Fig. 248).

Add Earth Powder beyond the area immediately around the stream's banks so that you can blend it in more convincingly with surrounding groundwork in later steps. Whilst the Earth Powder is being used on the stream bed, it is worth covering all

Fig. 250. Painted Raw Grass is fixed in place around the stream and paths. Neat PVA glue is used to hold it.

Fig. 251. A little bit of rubbish in streams like this can add to their effect.

the areas you want to represent as earth with the powder.

For the path, paint on a thick coat of dilute PVA and apply a light sprinkling of Treemendus Weathered Ballast, to give the path a little extra texture. Next, give it a sprinkling of Earth Powder (Fig. 249) and then spray the path with hairspray.

The majority of the groundwork will be covered in Raw Grass material. Trim pieces of the fabric to shape, to fit along the sides of the path and around the stream. Also trim them to length and subtly colour them using Sap Green paint (see Chapter 3). Paint PVA glue on to the bare plaster and fix the material to the plaster by pushing its backing into the glue (Fig. 250). Allow the glue to dry before neatening the edges using sharp scissors.

Any sign of the backing still visible once the excess has been trimmed away can be covered up with finely chopped Raw Grass fibres and Earth Powder.

Streams like the one portrayed here always seem to attract junk and this one is no different. A barrel and bicycle from P & D Marsh have been glued to

Fig. 252. Choose posters that are relevant to the era you are modelling. Such details make up the whole picture.

Fig. 253. Signs are a good way to brighten up fences and buildings.

the bed of the stream. A sheet of corrugated iron (the piece missing from the fence) is placed across the stream and acts as a short cut from one side to the other (Fig. 251).

Posters are great at adding character to walls, fences and buildings. Try to use posters that fit in with the era you are modelling, as this will help you to get the atmosphere right. There are hundreds of images from all different eras and regions available online, for you to print out. Make sure you scale them down to a suitable size and trim them out carefully. Paint a little glue directly on to the back of the poster and put it in position on the fence (Fig. 252). Fly posters are often put up in haste and when modelled look good if one or more of their corners are curled over and not glued to the fence.

Fig. 254. A small patch has been trimmed and coloured to represent an area of burnt grass. This effect can be used on railway embankments too.

Signs indicating the type of business behind the fence also add to the scene. They can be designed on a computer and printed out. To give them a more rigid look than the posters, stick them on thin card, trim them to size and then weather them to fit in with their surroundings. On the example, the signs have been stuck to posts, which will raise them above the fences of the yards (Fig. 253).

To give a realistic impression of a section of newly burnt grass (Fig. 254), trim a small patch very short and paint it black using poster paint. Leave the paint to dry and add a small amount of light dust pigment to the area to represent ash. Add a light sprinkling of fine scatter to the blackened patch to show that there is new growth returning. The scatter is held in place with a little diluted PVA glue and the whole patch is sprayed with hairspray, which will also hold the ash pigment in place.

The stream enters the scene from underneath the viaduct and from the little culvert on the right-hand side of the viaduct. To add some variety to the water in the stream it is possible to introduce stretches that are polluted either by local industry or a build-up of algae.

The pipe at the side of the stream was added in an earlier step before the plaster coating. To achieve a suitable rust colour, mix a little orange paint with

Fig. 255. Polluted water is added to the pipe that runs into the stream.

Making Waves water product from Deluxe Materials and add it to the end of the pipe to give the impression of water gushing out. The bed of the stream is also given a light coat of orange paint, following the flow of the water; this will be covered over with the water (Fig. 255).

Seal the bed of the stream using a thin layer of Scenic Water, varnish or neat PVA glue and allow it to dry. This will stop the top layer of tinted water soaking into the bed.

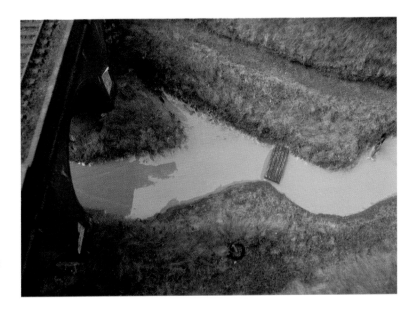

Fig. 256. Once it has been coloured, the resin gives a great effect of a slow-flowing dirty stream.

Fig. 257. Polluted water coming from the pipe is added to the surface of the resin as streaks.

The layer of resin added to the stream needs to be only 1–2mm in depth; for deeper water it is best to add it in two coats. Follow the instructions carefully when mixing two-part resins and avoid cross-contaminating the resin and hardener other than in the mixing vessel.

To create the dirty water present in the stream, mix the Solid Water two-part resin, this time with the addition of a couple of drops of a suitable coloured enamel or acrylic paint to give a cloudy look. Some of the mix is left clear and is poured into the channel towards the back of the scene, coming from the culvert before the paint is added.

The coloured resin is carefully poured along the length of the stream (Fig. 256).

Whilst the Solid Water is still wet and workable, orange paint is worked into it in little streaks flowing from the pipe and in line with where the overflow

Fig. 258. Tufts of weeds, long static grass fibres and fine scatter all add to the effect of plant life struggling to survive in the water.

Tip

Resins tend to 'creep' up the sides of stream beds, riverbanks and lakeside shores. If this happens, allow the resin to dry and apply a little glue over the offending area. Whilst the glue is still wet, cover it using a relevant scenic material that matches the rest of the bank. Be sure to create a neat edge between the water and the bank.

pipe sticks out from the bank. More paint can be added to the water to give the impression of further streaks according to your requirements. The effect can be enhanced if the orange paint is dragged using a cocktail stick or something similar along the length of the stream, to give the impression of a slow-flowing body of water (Fig. 257).

To add individual long static grass fibre tufts to the bed of the stream, wait until the resin has started to set, as this will help the fibres to stay fairly upright in the water. While the resin is still wet, fine scatter may also be added to small areas, to represent plants growing along the edge of the stream and weeds growing around features in the stream (Fig. 258).

A small piece of Seamoss is sprayed with a mid-toned grey/brown paint and left to dry. Once it is dry, spray the structure with hairspray and sprinkle Treemendus fine Mid Summer scatter on to the fine 'branches'. Avoid getting any scatter on the trunk and thicker branches as this can look unrealistic; to get the best results, take your time and only add scatter to the fine branch tips. The tree is then sprayed with Treemendus Scenefix glue to fix the scatter in place. A small hole is drilled into the baseboard and the tree is inserted (Fig. 259), held in place with glue if necessary.

THE COMPLETED DIORAMA

Even in rural areas of the UK, scenes such as this (Fig. 260) are not uncommon. A stream appears from the shadow of a railway viaduct and is immediately filled with dirty waste water from the coal and tarmac yards at the top of the slope. The fences around the yards display the name and nature of the businesses they protect and fly posters adorn the fences too. Rubbish, pollutants and algae are present in this stretch of stream for a short distance until once again it starts picking up speed as it heads towards a lake.

Fig. 259. Small trees often grow alongside streams and can be interesting features in scenes like this.

SUMMARY

Model railways built on split levels give you an opportunity to include bridges, steep embankments or viaducts. The only part of the scene that is on the same level as the track on the baseboard is the track running across the viaduct. Everything below the viaduct can be treated as a piece of model landscaping in its own right without having to take any of the other features of the layout into account.

Fig. 260. Streams on model railways work well whether the water is clean or dirty and should be modelled to suit the environment through which they run. By creating streams that go out of sight and reappear elsewhere on the layout, continuity in the landscape can be achieved.

CHAPTER NINE

NATURAL LAKES

Fig. 261. A natural lakeside setting complete with grass, mud and plants of all shapes and sizes.

Materials

- Emulsion paints
- Polystyrene
- Thick card
- Scenic modelling materials
- PVA glue
- Clear varnish
- Paints/weathering powders

Tools

- Steel rule
- Scalpel/Stanley knife
- Large paintbrush

A lake is a large area of water surrounded by land and not generally connected to the sea, except sometimes by a river or stream. Some lakes are formed naturally in deep basins and fissures on the Earth's surface.

The lake and the lakeside in the example are easy to build. It is a tranquil scene, somewhat overgrown, with an abundance of bushes, brambles, weeds and reeds. There are plants and greenery of all sizes and shades on the edge of the lake, blending into the surrounding area.

The methods described for making the plants and greenery that grow in such areas can be used for plants anywhere on your layouts.

PLANNING AND PREPARATION

A long thin lake, of the sort that can often appear naturally in the landscape, is easier to fit in to the scenery of most model railway layouts. Because of its shape, it can be designed to take up considerably less space than a more rounded lake.

In the initial planning stages, there are a number of methods to consider when incorporating a lake into the baseboard. One way is to draw the shape of the lake on to the baseboard and cut it out with a jigsaw. The resulting hole then has a 'floor' added to the bottom of the baseboard, creating a deep hollow, and the banks can then be fashioned to meet the existing level of the baseboard. This will result in fairly deep banks around your lake.

A second, simpler option involves building the edges or banks of the lake up from the baseboard – only a small bank is necessary to give a good impression of a natural-looking lakeside. When using the second option, the water's surface can be painted directly on to the baseboard and there is no need to cut any of the board away. The painted surface can then be covered with a number of materials to represent the water. Two-part resins, clear varnish, PVA or clear acetate are all useful, depending on the look of water you want to achieve.

The lake in the example, which is modelled using the second option, measures 600 x 210mm overall (approximately 24in at its longest and 8in wide at its widest). Start by planning out the shape and size of the lake, using a pencil or marker pen, directly on to the baseboard. You may want to draw it on a large piece of paper first to make sure you are happy with its shape and size. It may also be useful at this point to mark any other features you want to add, to determine whether they will all fit into the space available. These features might include a small jetty, a stream feeding the lake with water, an island in the lake, a road or even a railway line either passing near to or even crossing the lake via a bridge of some sort. In the example (Fig. 262), there is a narrow tributary feeding fresh water into the lake.

STARTING CONSTRUCTION

When creating lakes that are not sunken into the landscape but actually painted on to the flat surface of the baseboard, as here, it is possible to give the impression of deep water using a simple painting technique. The deepest parts of the lake, generally towards the centre, are painted with darker colours, in this case almost black matt emulsion. The areas closer to the edges are painted using progressively

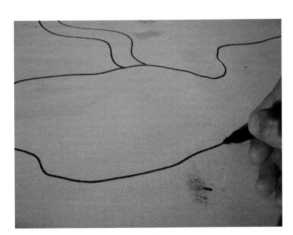

Fig. 262. Marking the outline of the lake and other features on the baseboard helps you to visualize how it will fit within the layout.

Fig. 263. Painting darker colours towards the centre of the lake will give an impression of deeper water. Lighter colours around the perimeter will look shallower.

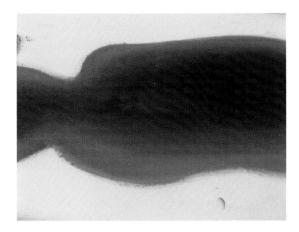

Fig. 264. Painting beyond the outline will help blend the water in with the shore.

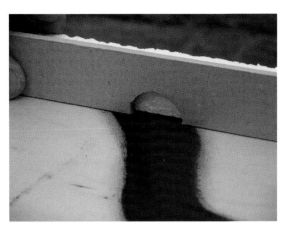

Fig. 265. A small tributary is added for greater interest.

lighter tones of brown, green and earth-coloured matt emulsion paints, blended together to avoid obvious bands of different shades and colours. This painting technique will give the impression that the outer parts of the lake are shallower than the centre (Fig. 263).

This technique works exactly the same when creating canals, rivers and streams that are painted directly on to the baseboard.

Painting beyond the outline of the lake using the lightest-coloured paints will help with the blending in when the groundwork materials are added (Fig. 264).

To the rear of the lake is a wall behind which a train track runs. You may choose to put a road there instead if it is more appropriate to your layout. A half-inch high strip of polystyrene is used to raise the height of the track but a stronger timber alternative would be more suited to the running of trains. The idea behind raising the track in this scenario is so that a small culvert can be set underneath the height of the track and a small tributary will be seen feeding the lake with water. It is the little details such as these that will add more interest to your model railways.

Add a strip of card to the side of the polystyrene sheet, to hide it from view; this strip will become the wall (Fig. 265).

The pipe or pipes need not be large, indeed, some of them are quite tiny in diameter. Two narrow brass tubes will give a hint of pipes and will eventually be mostly covered over with scenic materials. Fix the pipes in place using glue (Fig. 266).

To create a channel for the water to run down, cut a thin piece of card in a shape that follows the course of the water painted on to the baseboard. The paint marking the tributary will actually be covered with groundwork materials ultimately. Trace the shape painted on the baseboard on to paper and then place

Fig. 266. Pipes are glued in place. Eventually, they will have water running from them.

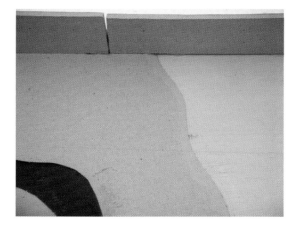

Fig. 267. Chamfering the edges of the card will make it easier to blend into the rest of the groundwork.

Fig. 268. The wall is painted and weathered to suit its surroundings.

this on the card and cut round it to ensure that all the desired shapes meet. Cut all the edges of the card to give them a chamfer, then glue the card to the board (Fig. 267). The edges of the card will eventually be hidden with scenic modelling materials and the chamfer helps with the blending-in process. The thicker the card, the deeper the channel will appear.

The card wall to the rear of the lake is covered in an embossed foam sheet, which is easily fixed in place with a glue such as PVA. Once the walling is fixed it can be painted and dry brushed, to pick out

Fig. 269. The lakeside is given an undercoat of emulsion paint and the shape of the lake is refined.

the detail of the individual courses of stone. Capping stones can be made from thick card, then glued to the top of the wall and painted using the same process as the wall itself (Fig. 268).

The wall being made at the rear of the lake will eventually be covered and obscured with lots of plants and most of it will not be on view. If this is the case on your layout, you do not need to go to too much effort with your painting at this stage.

Walls can of course be built away from the layout and added when they are complete.

Add a coat of natural beige matt emulsion paint to the baseboard (Fig. 269), to act as a good base for the groundwork materials. Any small areas that do not have scatters or other materials adhered to them will have a suitable base colour showing through. Alternatively, green or dark brown can be used for this undercoat. One match pot of emulsion paint will go a long way and can be diluted with a drop of water for better coverage if required.

Use this coat of emulsion to define the edge of the lake. Blending it into the paint already on your baseboard will ensure a natural-looking progression from the shore to the shallowest water around the perimeter of the lake. Do not be too worried about any little splashes or imperfections as these can be covered up in later steps.

ADDING GROUNDWORK

Begin by adding the groundwork materials to the channel coming from the culvert. Use a paintbrush to paint a thick coat of PVA glue into the channel and sprinkle a blend of fine ballasts and gravel on to it. Add a little Treemendus Normandy Earth Powder to the centre of the channel, to represent the finer silt that can gather in such places (Fig. 270). The sides of the channel can be built up slightly at this point, using the glue and ballast, to give a deeper appearance to the channel.

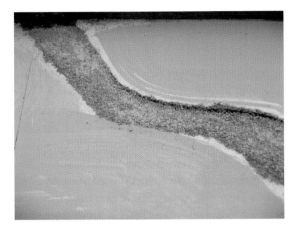

Fig. 270. Texture and colour are added to the bed of the tributary.

Give the terrain around the lake a coat of PVA, diluted 1 part PVA to 1 part water. Whilst the glue is still wet, give it a light coating of Treemendus Earth and Normandy Earth Powders. The Normandy Earth is also used around the lake, where it is useful for building the banks up slightly to create a difference in the ground and water level. To further enhance the effect (Fig. 271), apply a bead of diluted PVA around the edge of the lake, using a bottle with a nozzle fitted. Immediately drop pinches of the Normandy Earth into the glue, which will soak up the glue and create the bank. Adding a sprinkling of Earth Powder on top of the banks in certain areas will add variety in the colour once the glue has dried. Leave the banks to dry before adding more scenic materials to the groundwork.

Note the bank is only an inch or so wide around the lake and need not continue further out into the baseboard.

Next, paint a thin coating of diluted PVA over the ground surrounding the lake (not the lake itself). Whilst the glue is wet, add some of the fine ballast used in the channel to the groundwork around the lakeside (Fig. 272), to add further texture to the groundwork. A blast of hairspray at this point will help it adhere to the previous layer of groundwork.

Various colours of scatter are also added to the groundwork at this stage. Fresher, brighter greens will be found nearer to the water, both at

Fig. 271. The edge of the lake is given a slight bank, which really adds to the look of the lakeside.

Fig. 272. Texture is added to the lakeside.

Fig. 273. Scatters add a base colour to the groundwork ahead of the main plants.

Fig. 274. Static grass is used in patches around the lakeside. When applying the glue, it is best to work in small patches at a time.

the lakeside and along the edge of the tributary (Fig. 273). Use both fine and coarser grades of scatter, to add variety to the lakeside. When you are happy with the amount of scatter on the groundwork, spray the whole area with hairspray and allow it to dry, then vacuum up any loose scenic materials before the next step is undertaken.

Adding static grass fibres around the lakeside and around the tributary will give even more variety to colour and texture of the groundwork. For the best

results, apply the static grass glue on to the baseboard using a half-inch paintbrush in the places where you want the grass to be 'growing'. Remember, working in smaller patches at a time is better than painting a vast area with glue all in one go (Fig. 274).

When it comes to using the applicator, try screwing a small metal hook into the baseboard by hand, to provide an attachment for the applicator's crocodile clip. Using the Noch Gras-Master applicator, add short static grass fibres (such as Noch Spring

Fig. 275. Short static grass fibres are added to the glue, then more glue is added to the groundwork to hold longer fibres in place.

Fig. 276. Long static grass fibres are added to the fresh glue. They will also stick to the tiny gaps in between the short fibres.

Meadow 1.5mm) to the glue. Follow the instructions supplied with the applicator, making sure the correct sieve is used for the length of fibres chosen. Setting up the Noch Gras-Master correctly will yield the best results possible.

Apply further glue over some areas of the short fibres and around the patches of fibres to allow for the addition of longer grasses (Fig. 275). Whilst the glue is still wet, add Noch Wildgras XL (12mm) fibres and the relevant sieve to the applicator. These fibres are then applied on to the fresh glue and over the patches already covered with short fibres. There will be tiny spaces between the short fibres which allow for the longer fibres to be fixed to the glue, giving the grass some variety in height and colour (Fig. 276).

Applying different lengths and colours of fibres to the same area gives a far more realistic-looking result than using just one length and colour of fibre, which can look a little manicured. This is especially important when creating a natural-looking terrain is the objective.

A third application, this time of medium-length grass fibres, can then be introduced to the groundwork. Adding Noch Wild Grass beige (6mm) fibres on to and in between the patches of grasses already in place will start to help to blend the whole scene

together. A light sprinkling of Earth Powder between the fibres stops the shine from the glue, which may sometimes be visible showing through (Fig. 277).

Allow the groundwork to dry before vacuuming up all the loose fibres and Earth Powder.

The next step is to add Noch static grass tufts to the edge of the lake, including a few glued in place just inside the lake, which will look like they are growing out of the water once it has been added. The rest have been placed in position right on

Fig. 277. Medium-length fibres may be introduced; they will help blend all the patches of groundwork together.

Fig. 278. Colourful static grass tufts are fixed around the edges of the lakeside.

Fig. 279. Rocks and boulders are carefully positioned around the lakeside. Ideally, they should be of the same type as any other rock in the vicinity.

Fig. 280. Rubberized horsehair brambles are fixed around the lake, while larger rubberized horsehair shrubs are 'planted' close to the wall.

the water's edge and along the tributary. A small dab of glue to their base is enough to hold them in place (Fig. 278).

A natural lakeside may have boulders around its shores and small boulders and rocks may be added to the groundwork at this stage (Fig. 279). Take some of the small chunks of painted plaster that were made for a previous project (Chapter 5) and fix them in place with a spot of glue.

The lakeside in the example is set in a fairly natural and overgrown setting. Brambles made using rubberized horsehair covered with scatters of various colours are finely chopped and worked into the shoreline around the lake. Blend them so they fit naturally with the static grass and other scenic materials already in place. A few large rubberized horsehair shrubs can also be added to the rear of the scene (Fig. 280), held in place by a spot of glue. Spray them

Tip

It is helpful to imagine the various scenic elements described here being modelled together in various combinations on a single layout. For example, the boulders around the lake are the same rocks that were used on the hillside model (Chapter 5), and this lake would look good at the foot of the rocky hillside, with a railway line running between the two features. The two areas could then be unified by the use of grasses of the same colour and rocks of the same composition, whether they are sandstone, limestone or granite, and so on.

Fig. 281. Finer-textured bushes and shrubs complement the texture of the rubberized horsehair. These are made using a synthetic hair and Treemendus scatters.

Fig. 282. Noch laser-cut plants are easy to use and very effective.

lakeside up against the wall (Fig. 281). A little PVA will hold them in place.

If you want to add plants, there are a huge variety of species available in the Noch laser-cut range. The plants are laser-cut from pre-printed paper and do not need to be painted. Carefully remove them from the sheet by cutting with a very sharp blade or by tearing the paper around them away (Fig. 282). The plants need to be folded to shape before use and are easily fixed to the groundwork with a small spot of glue (Fig. 283). Plants and flowers tend to look best when planted in groups of the same species rather than dotted around the landscape, although any planting scheme is very much up to the individual.

THE WATER

The deep-water effect for the lake is achieved both by the colour of paint used on the surface of the baseboard and the materials used to represent the water. The end result of this technique is the impression of water that is slightly choppy as lake water can appear on breezy days.

The first step in transforming the base colour of emulsion paint into realistic-looking water is to give the painted area of the baseboard a thin coat of neat

lightly with Scenefix glue and hairspray once they are in position around the lake.

A similar effect can be achieved using Canopy, a synthetic hair supplied as a plait. It is fine enough to allow for bushes and shrubs with tiny branches to be produced. Tease the material into open airy structures, spray with hairspray and cover with assorted fine scatters. The bushes or shrubs are then sprayed with Scenefix glue and hairspray and placed on to the

Fig. 283. Groups of bulrushes and iris surround the tributary.

Fig. 284. A thin layer of clear varnish seals the baseboard and protects the paint on the bed of the lake.

Fig. 285. A thick layer of PVA glue is painted over the base coat of varnish and stippled as it dries.

PVA glue or clear varnish. This seals the coat of paint and the porous surface of the baseboard, in this case wood, and allows the next steps to be undertaken without fear of the baseboard soaking up the additional layers of 'water'. The PVA or clear varnish is applied using a brush and carefully painted right up to the edge of the lake (Fig. 284). For the seal coat it is possible to use a quick-drying clear varnish, which goes on milky but dries to a clear finish. It is important to let this layer dry completely before carrying on with the next step.

To create depth and texture to the water in the lake, paint a thick coat of PVA glue directly over the dry varnish on the baseboard. To give the surface of the water a slightly choppy appearance, texture the coat of glue using a stiff-bristled

Fig. 286. A top coat of varnish is applied over the dry PVA. Weeds can be added at this stage and the varnish will hold them in place once it has dried. The varnish is still wet here.

Fig. 287. Extra texture in the water can be added around the shoreline if required.

Once the glue has dried, the surface of the lake can be given a thin coat of clear varnish, applied using a good-quality soft brush. The varnish will add more of a shine to the surface of the lake and therefore improve the overall look of the water's surface. Try to avoid any dust settling on the varnish as it dries.

The previous step of adding a layer of stippled PVA and varnish may be repeated and can give the effect of deeper water, but is not always necessary.

Detail may be added by carefully placing laser-cut water lilies on to the surface of the varnish whilst it is still wet and sprinkling a little fine scatter in small patches to represent weeds at the surface of the water. Cutting the lower legs off a Noch angler figure and fixing it in the water near to the edge of the lake tricks the eye into thinking that he is standing in deep water as opposed to a thin layer of glue (Fig. 286).

Applied around some parts of the lake, Deluxe Materials Making Waves can be used to add more texture to the edges and give the impression of small ripples on the shore. Applied with a thin paintbrush, Making Waves goes on white but dries to a clear finish. When it has dried, try painting over it with white emulsion paint, to add tiny white waves around the shore (Fig. 287).

decorator's paintbrush. The process of adding the texture involves stippling the glue with the bristles of the brush as it dries (Fig. 285). The glue will have a tendency to settle flat but by repeating the stippling action whilst the glue is drying you will achieve a very realistic effect to the water.

The glue will be white as it is applied to the baseboard but as it dries it will be clearer.

Fig. 288. Clear varnish is added to the tributary to represent the water flowing into the lake.

Fig. 289. The impression of moving water can be created using Deluxe Materials Making Waves and white emulsion paint.

Clear varnish is also used to add a water effect into the channel, being carefully poured along the channel leading from the culvert to the lake (Fig. 288). To get water into narrow channels such as this one it can be advisable to use a syringe or allow it to drip off a thin strip of wood or a wooden skewer. Allow it to dry. Paint Making Waves on to the clear varnish in the channel and also around parts of the shoreline and surface of the water where the water from the channel joins the lake. A little white emulsion paint can then be painted on to the Making Waves to add to the impression of the movement in the water (Fig. 289).

Fig. 290. Early morning as the sun rises over the lake. The lighting shows the ripple effect on the surface of the water to great effect.

THE COMPLETED DIORAMA

The choppy effect of the water, created by using clear varnish and PVA glue, can be clearly seen in the completed layout. The narrow lake is surrounded by plenty of lush growth and plant life, all of which add to the natural look of the landscape. Adding streams, tributaries or lakes to your scenery will give your landscapes a very important element: water. Once you have incorporated water, you will be able to introduce other features associated with it, such as bridges, culverts, jetties, boats and even fishermen (Fig. 290).

SUMMARY

A lake need not be a huge feature – indeed, they are often fairly long and narrow, and this will enable you to introduce one fairly easily to your layout. If you plan in advance, you will be able to have a road leading to your lake, but you will need to consider this before construction begins. The water can be created by using relatively inexpensive and readily available materials and its colour is determined by the choice of paint used in the early steps of its production. Deeper water is represented by using darker paint.

Fig. 291. On prestigious duties, 55 022 hauls a special twelve-coach passenger train through stunning scenery. The colours of the lake, grasses and shrubbery in the foreground are a good representation of the more muted tones of the back scene.

CHAPTER TEN

MAINTAINED LAKESIDES

Fig. 292. A real lake that is used for recreation. The edges are protected by rustic poles set vertically to stop the action of the water eroding the paths around it.

Materials

- Thick card/ply
- PVA glue/superglue
- Plastic strip/basswood/balsa wood
- Embossed sheet/wooden skewers/ cocktail sticks
- Scenic modelling materials
- Emulsion paint

Tools

- Steel rule
- Scalpel/Stanley knife
- Large paintbrush

This carefully maintained lake, which is used for recreation, can be reached by car and has a hedge-lined car park on its shore. There are a number of processes involved in making a neat and tidy lakeside and realistic water's edge. Some lakes, like the one in Chapter 9, occur naturally and they are more likely to have a wild, somewhat overgrown look. Other lakes are man-made, created following the excavation of earth for use elsewhere, in the construction of embankments for example. The resulting pit may be filled by diverting water from a nearby river, or simply left to fill naturally. Such lakes are often put to good use for recreation.

Man-made lakes can be massive and modelling one in its entirety will probably take up far more space than is available on the average layout. Often it is more practical to model just a small section of lake, giving a hint of its overall size. Either way, the following techniques may also be used to create ponds and smaller bodies of water.

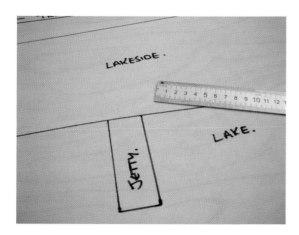

Fig. 293. As with most projects you undertake on your layout, good planning is essential. Measuring and drawing the features can highlight any flaws in the design at an early stage.

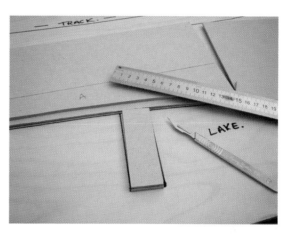

Fig. 294. Creating a difference between the water and ground level can be easily achieved using thick card or ply.

This project would make a nice feature at the front of a layout, with just a hint of the water visible but much of the lakeside showing. If the lakeside is modelled over a long stretch of the available baseboard it will give a good impression of being the edge of a much larger body of water. The techniques involved can also be applied to canals and docks, or even a stretch of coastline.

PREPARATION

Even if the body of water you are modelling is not going to be a whole lake surrounded by land, it is important to create an area large enough to give an impression of being part of a much larger body of water.

The outline of the lake is initially drawn on to 3mm thick card and carefully cut out with a sharp blade. The card is then positioned on the baseboard and the lake's outline traced on to the baseboard using a magic marker or pencil. Be sure to include a slight curve to the outline of your section of lake, to achieve a realistic look. Straight lines will give the impression of a canal as opposed to the edge of a lake.

At this early stage it is good practice to mark any other features – the position of the railway line, the

lane, the entrance to the lake and the car park – on to the baseboard (Fig. 293).

Raising the front of the card will give greater height between the water level and the surrounding ground level. To do this, trace again around the curved outline cut from the card but this time not directly on to the baseboard but on to a new piece of 3mm card. Very carefully cut along the curved line drawn on the card. Cut the back of the card using a blade and a steel rule to give you a strip of card with

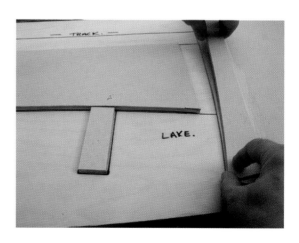

Fig. 295. Doubling the thickness of the card using carefully trimmed strips glued to the main pieces.

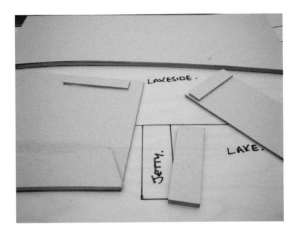

Fig. 296. All the pieces of 'lakeside' are now trimmed and prepared and ready to fix in place on the layout.

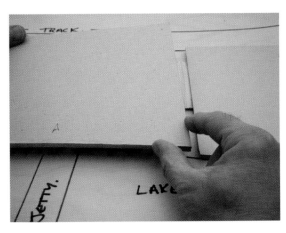

Fig. 297. PVA glue is used to fix the raised lakeside to the baseboard.

a shaped edge at the front. Repeat this until all the sections of card cut for the lakeside have a similar strip that mirrors them. Cut two card strips for use as the jetty (Fig. 294).

The corresponding pieces of card are fixed together using PVA glue or similar (Fig. 295). Be sure to get the edges to line up as near as possible, as this will assist you in a later step. This is a great way of introducing small differences in the levels on your layout. Put a weight on top of the card if necessary until the glue sets.

The rear of the card sections, which will become the lakeside, have had narrow card strips glued to them to hold the lakeside horizontal. As a result, the whole lakeside is raised 6mm from the baseboard (Fig. 296). Of course the lakeside can be made to slope gently down to the lake if more layers of card strips are added to raise the rear edge of the lakeside.

The lakeside terrain can now be fixed to the baseboard. This may be easier if the individual pieces of card are joined together at this stage (unless of course you have used a larger sheet to create your lakeside). This can be done by gluing a strip of card to the edge which butts up to the neighbouring piece of card. Glue is added to the top of this strip as the pieces are glued on to the baseboard (Fig. 297). Use a little glue on the strips of card to fix the lakeside to the layout and hold them down with weights whilst the glue dries.

Paint the bed of the lake at this point with very dark emulsion paint (Fig. 298). This will provide a base for the detailing of the water's edge inside the lake, which will be more extensive than on the natural lake in Chapter 9. The top of the jetty is also painted at this stage.

Fig. 298. The bed of the lake is painted with emulsion paint in preparation for the detailing.

ADDING DETAIL

The edge of the lake needs dressing to hide the exposed card used to raise the ground level around it. Very fine corrugated card is perfect to achieve the desired effect and is quick and easy to trim and glue in place. Another option is to cut cocktail sticks into suitable lengths and glue them vertically along the edge of the card – this method is time-consuming, but a very nice result can be achieved.

Fig. 299. To emulate the edges of the prototype lake, corrugated card is painted and weathered prior to cutting. Planks are also prepared for the top of the jetty.

Painting the card before fixing it on to the lakeside is recommended but not essential. Here some thin strips of basswood have been trimmed into random thicknesses, to provide the planking on top of the jetty (Fig. 299). The dark coat of paint on the jetty will show through any gaps left between the pieces of basswood.

The corrugated card is measured and very carefully trimmed to the correct height – 6mm will bring it flush with the top of the card edging along the lakeside, so cut it to approximately 7mm high, to create a little lip to the very edge. The lip of corrugated cardboard will be made roughly flush with the groundwork at a later stage as the scenic materials are added. Glue the card and basswood in place (Fig. 300). At this stage, the planking on top of the jetty runs flush with the edging around the lake.

Buying ready-made fencing is a quick and easy way to add detail to your layout, with many styles available to suit most eras. Originally light grey plastic, their appearance can be improved with just a couple of light coats of paint (Fig. 301). The fences could be painted with matt white paint straight from an aerosol can and left looking freshly painted, to fit in with the maintained look of the lakeside; another option would be to paint them to represent wood. Two or more thin coats of paint will give a better result than one heavy coat of paint.

Fig. 300. The lakeside edging and jetty planks are glued in place. The planks will be enhanced in a later step.

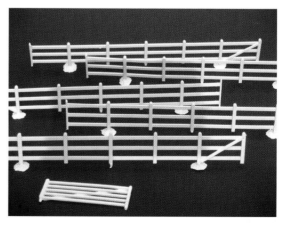

Fig. 301. Plastic fencing requires only a couple of light coats of paint before it is ready to add to the layout.

Tip

Next time you are out and about, take a look at fences and note how often they are far from perfectly straight and upright. Fences are often damaged by seasonal weather conditions, animals, people or vehicles, and, if you model them in this way, you will be adding to the realism of your layout. Fences on any layout should be weathered to suit their surroundings.

Fig. 302. Superglue holds the fencing in place.

By law, all British railway lines must be enclosed by fencing, so you will need to consider this when planning your layout. The fencing is supplied with pins on the bottoms of the posts and little plastic piles of earth into which the pins will fit. The piles of earth can be fixed to the bottom of the posts and then glued to the landscape. This method can be used where the bottoms of the posts will be hidden (Fig. 302). Alternatively, for a more realistic result, you can make small holes directly into the baseboard for the pins to sit in, fixing them with a little super-glue, and discard the little mounds of plastic.

The lane that leads to the lakeside car park is given a coat of Earth Powder. Before applying the glue that holds the powder in place, carve a few ruts and potholes out of the surface of the card using a sharp blade, to add extra detail to the lane's surface. Round off the edges of the carved areas by gently rubbing over them with fine-grade sandpaper.

To represent a tarmac surface in the car park, use a grey-coloured, fine-grade, between-coats sandpa-per, glued directly to the baseboard using PVA glue. You may need to persevere with the edges of the sheet and keep pushing them down until they are fixed; any joins or imperfections to the sandpaper add to the effect of the tarmac (Fig. 303). White lines showing the parking spaces could be added to the car park using a white pencil crayon. They do not

Fig. 303. The first steps of the groundwork include adding texture to the lane and creating the effect of tarmac in the car park.

Fig. 304. Blending the earth of the lane and tarmac of the car park gives an impression of the movement of traffic.

need to be pristine, unless you want them to look as if they have just been painted.

The join between the earth of the lane and the tarmac of the car park can be blended together with Earth Powder, to give the impression that the tyres of vehicles have dirtied the tarmac as they enter the car park from the lane.

Remember that the effect will be much more pleasing once the glue has dried.

Lanes like this have often had a couple of their potholes filled in with hardcore (Fig. 304). The effect of this can be achieved by the application of a tiny pinch of fine ballast, held in place with a drop of glue and a light spray of hairspray.

HEDGES

Neatly trimmed hedging borders the car park and one side of the lane leading to it. The hedges are very simple to make, using thin strips of rubberized horse-hair. Take a block of the material and cut enough strips to cover the length of hedging you require. If you want neat hedging, trim the strips carefully to keep them fairly uniform. If you want a more naturally shaped or overgrown hedgerow, the strips can be pulled and teased apart by hand. Position the basic structures for neat hedgerows on the layout, to ensure that the correct length of hedging is available before proceeding with the construction (Fig. 305).

The finished hedges will look better if the horsehair is given a light spray of a dark-coloured paint – any-thing from mid-brown to black, or even a bit of both (Fig. 306). The coat of paint does not have to be heavy or completely cover all the rubberized horsehair. Use just enough to tone it down a touch and to add depth and shade to the finished hedgerow. The paint can be left to dry before proceeding but you can continue with the next step straight away if you prefer.

Soak the 'hedge' with a generous amount of hair-spray and apply a scatter of a suitable colour – on

Fig. 305. Hedges made from thin strips of rubberized horsehair are checked in situ and trimmed to the correct length.

Fig. 306. The strips of rubberized horsehair are spray painted with black paint, to add depth and shade to the hedges.

Fig. 307. Applying hairspray, scatter and diluted PVA to the painted horsehair results in very robust, flexible hedges.

the example, Treemendus Mid Summer and a little Spring scatter represent fresh growth (Fig. 307). The amount of scatter you add to the horsehair can also affect how dense the hedge will appear – for example, adding less gives the impression of a newly trimmed hedge. To fix the scatter permanently, the whole hedge can be sprayed with a good soaking of a diluted PVA (1 part PVA to 4 parts water), using a bottle with an atomizer spray. The type of bottle that holds kitchen cleaner is very useful for this.

Put the hedges to one side and allow them to dry. Once they have dried, and before they are fixed to the layout, a nice effect can be created by trimming the bottoms at a slight angle to expose some of the horsehair, creating a narrower base. This means that the foliage starts a little above ground level, adding to the appearance of this particular type of hedge.

The hedges are held in place with neat PVA glue, which is best applied to the base of the hedge just before fixing to the baseboard. A little glue to the ends of the hedge where two separate hedges join will also help hold them together. You may find it necessary to use something to hold them square on the baseboard whilst the glue sets.

Blend the areas around the bottoms of the hedges into the groundwork using very finely chopped Raw Grass fibres, worked into place with a cocktail stick on to a thin layer of Scenefix glue (Fig. 308).

Fig. 308. The first layer of groundwork materials is glued to the baseboard. The area around the bottom of the hedges has been blended into the groundwork.

LAKESIDE GROUNDWORK

The first layer of groundwork materials applied to the baseboard comprises a thick coating of diluted PVA glue covered with Treemendus Earth Powder, Normandy Earth Powder and various fine scatters and short static grass fibres sprinkled on by hand. Allow this layer to dry.

The pathways that circle the lakeside are given a coat of very fine light brown ballast. Paint diluted PVA glue on to the course you want your path to follow (it may be useful to draw the path in advance on to the baseboard before adding the initial groundwork layer, so that the design can be altered if required before the materials are added to the lakeside). Sprinkle the ballast on to the glue and give it a light spray with hairspray (Fig. 309). If you want to add more detail, you could cover your paths using materials to represent bark, tarmac, gravel, decking, or a mixture of different materials.

As this man-made lake is used for recreation, the detail includes lots of colourful flowering shrubs, bushes and plant life, which have been planted for the visitors to enjoy. This gives the modeller an opportunity to introduce a bit of bright colour; so often, the model railway layout features the more subtle tones of the countryside, or the dull colours of the dirt and grime of an industrial setting.

The bushes are made using Treemendus Canopy material, teased apart to create open airy structures on to which hairspray and a scattering of green scatters are added. More hairspray is applied, then coloured scatters are added to resemble flowers. The 'rhododendrons' and 'azaleas' are then sprayed with Scenefix glue to hold the scatters in place. The bushes are 'planted' in raised flower beds created from the same corrugated card that was used to shore up the lakeside (Fig. 310). This adds to the impression of the lakeside being a maintained space. The bushes are held in position with a spot of neat PVA glue.

The groundwork along the paths may be planted with laser-cut plants, flowers and ready-to-use flowering tufts, held in place with a single drop of superglue. Planting in neat rows such as these should only ever be done in managed areas, never in nature!

Fig. 309. The paths that circle the lake are made using very fine ballast sprinkled on to diluted PVA.

Fig. 310. Flowering plants, shrubs and bushes add a splash of colour to the scene.

Low-growing ground-cover plants may also be added to the scene, made by sprinkling a blend of green and coloured scatter on to a bed of diluted PVA glue (Fig. 311).

It is up to you how much colour you add to areas like this. One thing to consider is that some coloured scatters can be very garish and should probably be used only sparingly. It is best to add just a little at a time, so that you can get an idea of the final effect.

Tip

Spraying the Canopy after it has been teased apart with suitably coloured aerosol paint, prior to spraying it with hairspray, will result in more rigid bushes. Handle them with care or, better still, make sure the paint is totally dry before applying the hairspray and scatters.

Fig. 311. Laser-cut plants and flowers make interesting features along the paths on the lakeside.

CREATING THE LAKE BED

Assuming that your lakeside set-up is being built towards the front edge of your layout, as in the example, it is important to raise the edges of the baseboard slightly around the lake, to stop your chosen water material disappearing over the edge. This may be done by supergluing thin strips of timber to the front and sides of the diorama base. However, on a model railway layout on legs raised above the floor, it would be better to run a horizontal strip of 3mm ply board 150mm deep along the whole length of the front edge of the baseboards. This should be held in place with panel pins and PVA glue and given a couple of coats of paint. The ply should be fixed so as to finish proud of the top of the boards and will act as a 'lip', to contain the water material (Fig. 312). The strip can be given a coat of paint once the glue has dried.

The bed of the lake will benefit from a coat of clear varnish, not only to seal the paint on the board but also to seal the surface of the board and stop any of the water products seeping into it. It is vitally important to apply adequate varnish around the join between the baseboard top and the edging that will contain the water (Fig. 313). You can either use a quick-drying varnish here or seal the gap with a very fine bead of proprietary sealant, if you prefer.

Whilst the varnish is still wet, take a small amount of sand, earth, fine gravel or other similar fine material, and sprinkle it along the very edge of the lake, right up to the rustic posts along the lakeside (Fig. 314). It is a good idea to use materials already present on the lakeside, as this will help create a balance between the lake and the surrounding land, especially as there are already numerous colours on the lakeside plants. Apply it more heavily along the very edge of the rustic posts and less heavily as you move into the deeper water away from the edge of the lake. This will give a good impression of the level of the lake bed getting deeper as it moves away from the shore. Push it into the varnish with your fingertip to make sure it beds in. Allow the varnish to dry.

Paint a second coat of varnish on top of the previous one. This will create more depth to the water as the layers are added. Little patches of scatter can be added on to the varnish, to represent the weed growing beneath the surface of the water (Fig. 315). Make sure the scatter is pushed into the varnish quite firmly, to stop it being dislodged when the final layer of water is added.

Whilst the second coat of varnish is wet, take some small pieces of stone, gravel, cork or similar material, and carefully place them into the varnish (Fig. 316). Position them carefully, pushing some of

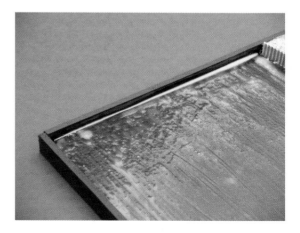

Fig. 312. It is important to enclose the edge of the lake. Here, strips of wood glued to the edge of the baseboard prevent the 'water' from running over the edge.

Fig. 313. Clear varnish seals the bed of the lake and the join between the top of the baseboard and the edging strip.

RIGHT: *Fig. 314. Texture and detail are added to the shallow parts of the lake.*

CENTRE RIGHT: *Fig. 315. A second coat of clear varnish and some green scatter are added to the lake bed.*

them into the scatter already in place. Try to avoid getting their tops covered in varnish as some of these rocks will be sticking out above the water level and look better 'dry' once the water has been added. Some of the smaller rocks will be visible just beneath the surface of the water.

Treemendus Sandstone Scree complements the brown ballast of the paths and the first layer of ballast laid down on the lake bed.

Fig. 316. Small rocks are very carefully added on to the wet varnish. Some of these will stick out above the surface of the water whilst others will be submerged.

Fig. 317. A rowing boat will make a nice feature to the lake.

A small boat is placed into the wet varnish at this stage. The bottom of this boat is perfectly flat and is another example of something that deceives the eye (Fig. 317). The observer is tricked into thinking that the water is deeper than it really is, because he imagines the boat to be fairly rounded at the bottom. The depth of the water in this lake will be only about 2mm.

Noch laser-cut bulrushes and iris are added in clumps around the edge of the lake, fixed in place with a small spot of superglue. Long static grass fibres are also added along the edge of the lake (Fig. 318). The jetty is purposely kept clear from plants and reeds.

Fig. 318. More detail is added to the lake in the form of laser-cut plants and long static grass fibres.

Fig. 319. Two-part resins result in extremely clear water, which allows the detail on the bed of the lake to show through.

Fig. 320. By creating a wake behind the rowing boat, movement is introduced on to the surface of the water.

ADDING THE WATER

Deluxe Materials Solid Water is used for the final layer of the water and will add depth to the lake; because it is crystal clear, it will allow the detailing below water level to be seen.

For the best results, measure 2 parts resin to 1 part hardener (use the syringes supplied in the pack for measuring small amounts, for example, for puddles; for larger amounts, pour the resin and hardener directly into the measuring beakers supplied). Adding extra hardener to the mix will not speed up the setting time of the resin.

When the components have been measured out, stir the contents until both parts are well mixed. Avoid introducing air into the liquid as this will create bubbles in the mix. When the mix is completely blended pour the resin into the sealed lake

Fig. 321. Small details such as these add meaning to the story being told within the scene.

bed. Use the spatula provided to work the resin into all the areas and gaps where you may want the 'water' to settle.

The drying time for this particular resin is approximately 24–36 hours. After 8–10 hours the resin can be stippled using a toothbrush or paintbrush with stiff bristles, to add ripples to the surface of the water. Alternatively, if you prefer, the resin can be left to dry perfectly flat to represent calm lake water (Fig. 319). You can also add a little movement to the water around the oars and hull of the rowing boat. This is done after the resin has dried, by using a little white emulsion paint to represent a slight froth (Fig. 320).

FINAL DETAILS

At the entrance to the car park a couple of postboxes and figures, from the P&D Marsh range of pre-painted white-metal model railway accessories, add a splash of colour. A tarpaulin-covered excavator adds another interesting feature to the scene (Fig. 321).

THE COMPLETED DIORAMA

It is a still, early summer's day and the surface of the water in the man-made boating lake is very calm and flat. The lake's edges are carefully maintained and kept in a fashion suitable for recreation, and a small jetty adds a special feature. The perimeter of the lakeside has been shored up with rustic wooden poles to stop erosion by the action of the water. Colourful flowering plants and bushes adorn the shore. Fishermen visit and swap 'You should have seen the one that got away' stories (Fig. 322).

This is a shallow lake and pebbles and weed can be seen under the surface of the water along its

Fig. 322. The distance between the front of the baseboard and the fence in front of the railway line is only approximately 250mm. Lakes modelled in this way take up very little space and can make interesting features in what may otherwise become wasted space at the front of a layout.

edges. A smartly painted fence separates the lakeside from the railway line that runs behind it – the branch line, which brings the summer hordes here to relax.

SUMMARY

This project shows how, with a fairly limited range of construction and scenic modelling materials, very realistic and diverse model scenery can be created.

It all depends on how the materials are used and made to work for you. It is clear in all the examples how colour can play a huge part in the way your models will be perceived, and this is something that the modeller should always bear in mind.

Some of the techniques can be a little fiddly, but none of the results are particularly difficult to achieve. By following the advice given here, you should discover new ways to improve not only your own modelling skills but also your layouts.

Fig. 323. End of the line. An unidentified Pannier tank engine stands idle awaiting its final journey. Next stop, the breakers.

USEFUL SUPPLIERS

AK INTERACTIVE
Weathering pigments and enamel paints
Europe website: ak-interactive.es
North America website: ak-interactive-usa.com

BACHMANN EUROPE PLC
Moat Way
Barwell
Leicester
Leicestershire
LE9 8EY
UK
Tel: 0870 751 9990
E-mail: sales@bachmann.co.uk
Website: www.bachmann.co.uk

DAPOL
Dapol Ltd
Gledrid Industrial Park
Chirk
Wrexham
LL14 5DG
UK
Tel: +44 (0) 1691 774455
E-mail: Shop@dapol.co.uk
Website: www.dapol.co.uk

DELUXE MATERIALS
Realistic water materials and modelling glues
E-mail: info@deluxematerials.com
Website: deluxematerials.com

DOVEDALE MODELS – Handmade buildings
David Wright
6 Ivy Court
Hilton
Derby
DE65 5WD
UK
Tel: +44 (0) 1283 733547
E-mail: david@dovedalemodels.co.uk
Website: www.dovedalemodels.co.uk

GAUGEMASTER
Gaugemaster Controls Ltd
Gaugemaster House
Ford Road
Arundel
West Sussex
BN18 0BN
UK
Tel: +44 (0) 1903 884488
E-mail: customerservices@gaugemaster.co.uk
Website: www.gaugemaster.com

HORNBY
Customer Care
Hornby Hobbies Ltd
Westwood Industrial Estate
Margate
Kent
CT9 4JX
UK
Tel: +44 (0) 1843 233525
E-mail: customercare@hornby.com
Website: www.hornby.com

id Backscenes
24 School Road
Telford
TF7 5JG
UK
Tel: +44 (0) 7970 678753
E-mail: info@art-printers.com
Website: www.art-printers.com

JAVIS MANUFACTURING LTD
Scenery maker, ready-to-use fences, drystone walls, Oxford Diecast and backscenes
JBB House, 6 Hammond Avenue
Whitehill Industrial Estate
Reddish
Stockport SK4 1PQ
UK
Tel: (+44)161 480 2002

E-mail: p-bridge@btconnect.com
Website: javis.co.uk
Trade sales only

METCALFE – Ready cut card kits
Bell Busk
Skipton
North Yorkshire
BD23 4DU
UK
Tel: +44 (0) 1729 830072
E-mail: info@metcalfemodels.com
Website: www.metcalfemodels.com

MODEL RAILWAYS DIRECT
Retail Unit 2, Phoenix Way
Portishead, Bristol
BS20 7GP
UK
Tel: +44 (0) 1275 774224
E-mail: sales@modelrailwaysdirect.co.uk
Website: www.modelrailwaysdirect.co.uk

PECO
PECO Technical Advice Bureau
Underleys
Beer
Devon
EX12 3NA
UK
Tel: +44 (0) 1297 21542
E-mail: info@pecobeer.co.uk
Website: www.peco-uk.com

NOCH
Static grass, Gras-Master applicator and laser-cut plants
Noch GmbH & Co. KG
Lindauer Straße 49
D–88239 Wangen im Allgäu
Germany

Tel: (+49) 7522 9780-28
Fax: (+49) 7522 9780–80
E-Mail: noch@noch.de
Website: noch.de or noch.com
Distributed in the UK by Gaugemaster Controls
Ltd., Arundel (gaugemaster.com)

P&D MARSH Model Railways
Pre-painted white-metal figures and accessories
The Stables
Wakes End Farm
Eversholt
Milton Keynes MK17 9FB
Tel: (+44)1525 280068
E-mail: paul@pdmarshmodels.com
Website: pdmarshmodels.com

SANKEY SCENICS
16 Norbreck Close
Great Sankey
Warrington
Cheshire
WA5 2SX
UK
Tel: +44 (0) 7565 892209
E-mail: sankeyscenics@live.co.uk
Website: www.sankeyscenics.co.uk

TREEMENDUS
Scenic modelling materials and hand-made trees
112 Church Lane
Ashton on Mersey
Sale
Cheshire M33 5QG
UK
Tel: (+44)161 973 2079
E-mail: info@treemendus-scenics.co.uk
Website: www.treemendus-scenics.co.uk

INDEX